We Are Not the Enemy

Restoring Honor

to U.S. Civil Service

Deborah D. Johnson

Mark E. Wallace

Copyright © 2013 by

Deborah D. Johnson and Mark E. Wallace.

All rights reserved.

Designed, illustrated, and published by

Aubey, LLC
Washington, D.C.

info@aubeyllc.com

www.aubeyllc.com

Edited by Holly Thesieres Monteith

ISBN: 1494355108
ISBN-13: 978-1494355104

To past, present, and future employees of the U.S. Civil Service and to concerned citizens with a heart for supporting its honorable and patriotic mission of serving the American public.

Civil servants always will have the American people's back despite dysfunctional politics.

— Al Gore

Contents

Preface i

Acknowledgements iii

Introduction 1

PART I: WE ARE NOT THE ENEMY

Chapter 1: Why This and Why Now? 9

Chapter 2: The Making of a Civil Servant 27

Chapter 3: The Road to the Senior Executive Service 35

PART II: RESTORING HONOR TO U.S. CIVIL SERVICE

Chapter 4: The Many Services Civil Service Workers Provide 45

Chapter 5: The Challenges of Civil Service Today 55

Chapter 6: Strategies for Meeting Today's Challenges 75

Chapter 7: Develop and Attract the Next Generation of Civil Service Leaders 93

Epilogue 110

Appendix: Informative Websites 116

Bibliography 119

About the Authors 121

Preface

In authoring this book, we drew on our own civil service experiences and the processes and perceptions we saw growing around us over our careers as federal employees.

Deborah grew up in the District of Columbia but never wanted a government job. She believed it would be boring and that it would not pay well, but she did not know much about working in the federal government. She considers herself fortunate to have had the opportunity to discover the reward that can be found as a civil servant as she worked for various federal agencies during summers in high school and college.

When she needed a full-time job, Deborah called on a former supervisor and obtained her first job as a career civil servant. Thirty years later, as she looks back and remembers the agencies she worked in and the people she worked for and with, she is proud to say that she was and always will be a civil servant. Although her work was challenging at times, she believes she made a difference.

Mark began working for the U.S. Census Bureau right out of college in the mid-1970s, retiring from the bureau at the end of 2012. He aspired to the ranks of the Senior Executive Service (SES), an elite corps of executives selected for their leadership qualifications. Mark served his last eleven and a half years in the SES and was proud to do so.

Looking back, there were good days and bad days, but there never was a dull day. Despite hearing an increasing amount of negative rhetoric about federal government workers as the years went by, Mark remained proud to be a civil servant. He always considered his employment with the federal government to be an honor and a privilege and believes that he left things in better shape than he found them.

As we concluded our public service in 2012, at a time when managing the public's business was never more important and the pursuit of excellence was never more needed to restore public confidence in our government, we both felt that we had retired under a dark cloud.

As civil servants, we did not consider ourselves as being part of a federal bureaucracy; we understood that we were under operating constraints that were different from private industry, but early on, we thought the tight rules were in place to protect public monies and the people whom the federal government serves. We were driven by the search for meaningful work, and we both felt we were fulfilling a noble calling through our service.

The recent targeting of the federal employee as lazy, wasteful and inefficient flies in the face of our own experiences serving the American public. We wrote this volume with the intent to inform the public of the truth of government service, advise how to attract and retain the most talented civil servants, and aid the public in safeguarding their own government through responsible citizenship.

Acknowledgements

We appreciate the many people who helped make this book possible through their encouragement, their constructive criticism, and the giving of their valuable time.

We especially thank Carol Bonosaro, president of the Senior Executives Association, for commenting on an early edition of this book and for providing guidance and expertise on critical issues that affect members of the SES and all federal employees.

We also give our thanks and appreciation to

Sarah Crim, (journalist and Bowie Interfaith Food Pantry volunteer), for insightful comments and advice on the manuscript;

Brian George, retired federal SES employee, for valuable guidance, direction, and encouragement at the launch of this book; and

Michael Coleman, pastor of the Reformed Presbyterian Church of Bowie, for providing encouragement and mentioning this book as part of a series of sermons based on Romans 13:1–7, calling us to be subject to governing authorities.

Numerous people we met along the way told us to go for it because this book is important at this time, inside and outside the Beltway.

We are thankful for the many dedicated men and women in the U.S. Civil Service who we knew and with whom we served over many years.

And of course, we are thankful for our spouses, children, parents, and extended families for their moral support and advice throughout this project.

Introduction

Working for the U.S. Civil Service was once honorable, but today, this is no longer so.

The deaths of four Americans—U.S. ambassador Christopher Stevens, former Navy SEALs Tyrone Woods and Glen Doherty, and computer expert Sean Smith—in the September 2012 terrorist attack on the U.S. Diplomatic Mission in Benghazi, Libya, indicated that government service is an important and sometimes hazardous duty. Yet, although four dedicated federal employees gave their lives, the public sector came under attack during election year 2012 in a way that not only marginalized their sacrifice and the inherent value of government service but also misrepresented and undermined the role of government in our society.

A partial government shutdown, from October 1 to October 16, 2013, forced hundreds of thousands of U.S. Civil servants to stay home. This event came on the heels of harmful sequester cuts during 2013 and a three-year pay freeze. Needless to say, many federal civil servants felt under-appreciated. It was ironic that a Pew Research Center study performed during these weeks found, by more than a two-to-one ratio among those surveyed, that the public liked federal workers.

Of the 1,504 people surveyed, from October 9 to 13, sixty-two percent said they had a favorable view of federal workers. There was another interesting finding: Congress was rated favorably by just 23 percent in the survey. We feel that this is an important distinction, especially since it is easy, and common, for the public to lump the whole federal government together in stating their views.

This book is meant for those who want to get rid of the federal government. It was also written for those who want to become better informed about what federal agencies and their employees do and why they do it. This book will help you better understand the president's and Congress' roles and responsibilities in ensuring a smooth and efficiently run government. It will enable you to grasp the scope of each U.S. citizen's basic civic duty, which is to be informed and engaged in the conduct of our democracy. Most important, this book will help us all understand why a civil service career is a worthy and rewarding calling.

Today, as we prepare the next generation of the nation's workforce, we are not doing enough to advance the U.S. Civil Service as a viable choice for individuals looking for meaningful work—for those who truly want to make a difference in the health, safety, security, well-being, and prosperity of our society. What's more, on the basis of key findings from studies of existing federal employees, there has been a recent alarming decrease in the number of mid-level managers aspiring to top leadership positions in the Senior Executive Service (SES). Barring significant improvements, none of this bodes well for the future of the U.S. Civil Service or, for that matter, of our great nation.

It may be easy to group the whole federal government together (civil servants and government leaders) in blaming a faceless bureaucracy as inefficient and a waste of money. That's what many folks "outside the beltway" do.

By this perception, a career as a civil servant is a waste of money—because civil servants are paid, federal funding does not get used effectively. We don't agree. Rather, as federal money becomes tighter and tighter, civil servants take on multiple roles and duties as other civil servants leave and are not replaced. They are asked by leadership in the executive and legislative branches of government to continue to perform all their duties with fewer and fewer resources. The public calls on civil servants for help. Individuals and companies use federal work for their own research and to answer questions. Of course, there is some wasteful spending, but what organization does not engage in wasteful spending, ever? Wasteful spending can happen in any organization that is managed by people. It is not the nature of the federal government alone. It is the nature of people in organizations operating amid suboptimal systems.

It has become trendy today for some to stereotype federal workers as lazy, inefficient, and incompetent bureaucrats. This was not what we saw in the places we worked. We saw people who worked for the federal government not because it was easy, or because they received a big paycheck, but because they valued the importance of their work. They cared about the missions of their agencies and their service to the nation. We saw dedicated workers who got satisfaction from making a difference in serving our nation.

Who defends the civil servant? The great majority of civil servants work hard, are dedicated to their duties, and consider public service to be a noble calling. However, blaming the government or federal employees for the ills of our society is the easy way out for some. And federal employees are easy marks because they can't defend themselves. But think about this: where would we be, really, without the contributions of the American civil service workers? And wasn't it odd that during the October 2013 shutdown that the public got such a better appreciation for the services of the federal workforce? As President Obama remarked on October 16 as the shutdown came to a close, "We hear all the time about how the government is the problem. Well it turns out we rely on it in a whole lot of ways. So let's work together to make government work better, instead of treating it like an enemy or purposely making it worse."

Furthermore, the ranks of the SES are being depleted. The keystone of the Civil Service Reform Act of 1978, the SES was established to lead the continuing transformation of government by serving as the link between presidential appointees and the rest of the federal workforce. In the 1980s, in the 1990s, and in 2001, when Mark entered the SES, such jobs were prestigious positions considered worth aspiring to. However, today, studies show that approximately 64 percent of the nearly seventy-one hundred senior executives will be eligible to retire by 2016, while the same studies show that the number of highly qualified candidates in the pipeline to replace retiring senior executives may not be adequate to fill agency vacancies. According to survey results, mid-level and upper-level managers in the federal government are less likely to aspire to positions in the ranks of the SES than they had over the last three decades. *Why is this*? This book seeks to answer this question.

At this juncture, it is important to clarify that this book is in no way intended to advance a liberal or a conservative approach to moving forward; rather, our intent is to speak up on behalf of federal employees who have worked under both

Democratic and Republican administrations over multiple years and are essentially nonpartisan on the job. In the words of John F. Kennedy, "let us not seek the Republican answer or the Democratic answer, but the right answer. Let us not seek to fix the blame for the past. Let us accept our own responsibility for the future."

Maybe we can find the answers to our questions in the pages that follow as we recount our careers and review some little known U.S. history. And maybe we can envision some next steps we all might take to restore the honor and legitimacy of federal employment in general and the SES in particular.

Federal service is a career path that does, indeed, have bumps in the road, but it is a path worth taking. We hope you travel this road with us.

PART I

WE ARE NOT

THE ENEMY

Chapter 1
Why This and Why Now?

> My fellow Americans, ask not what your country can do for you, ask what you can do for your country.
>
> —John F. Kennedy

The Pendleton U.S. Civil Service Reform Act of the United States was passed in 1883, during the Chester A. Arthur administration, in response to illegal activities by certain government officials. This law established the Civil Service Commission to enforce the merit system, whereby government jobs were given based on a person's ability instead of a person's politics. Prior to that, government jobs were often given as rewards for political loyalty, a practice that had resulted in widespread fraud and corruption.[1]

The Pendleton Act transformed the nature of public service. From that time through the mid-1960s, many well-educated and well-trained professionals found a rewarding career in U.S. federal service. It was an honor to be a civil  servant. Federal employees were respected. Civil Servants believed they did important work in serving the American people, and the people appreciated it.

But something disturbing has happened over the last few decades. The work of the U.S. Civil Service is the same: serving America. Yet today, although the work is still honorable, it is no longer honored.

Over the years, public trust in the government has eroded. At the end of the Eisenhower administration in the late 1950s, nearly three-quarters of Americans said they trusted the government to "do what is right" most of the time. Today, that's only 26 percent, according to a Pew survey done in January 2013. You could say there are good reasons for this erosion of trust: the Vietnam War, Watergate, President Clinton's impeachment hearing, the wars in Iraq and Afghanistan, the IRS scandal targeting politically affiliated nonprofits, and today's more-than-ever polarized political system, among others. These events have caused Americans to lose confidence in the government's ability to do its job. But the blame for these political maneuvers has been put onto the backs of civil service employees, and as a consequence, government service itself, crucial as it is, does not receive the respect that it deserves.

Indeed, leadership at various levels is making decisions that are having poor outcomes in government. But instead of blaming the leaders responsible for these outcomes, the public is blaming the civil service worker. This is neither right nor fair. Instead, the public should recognize that the civil servant is working for the public good, but can only work within the framework created by government leaders. Therefore, rather than blaming civil service workers for the government's ills, the public has the responsibility to ensure that its elected leaders are doing their job.

From our standpoint, the root causes of this problem are three main areas in which the public is not receiving accurate information. The way we see it, today the tax-paying general public is considerably uninformed and misinformed about the following:

- The valuable work done by federal employees and why they do it

- Political leaders' roles and responsibilities in ensuring a smooth and efficiently run federal government—and the fact that federal employees are getting unfairly blamed for the failure of political leaders to do their jobs

> The truth is that federal employees do provide essential and crucial services on a daily basis. And these valuable services are provided at a small fraction of the federal budget.

- The individual citizen's very own role and responsibility to be an informed and engaged citizen, dutifully participating in the conduct of our government

Because of this widespread lack of accurate information about the nature and importance of government service, many of our nation's citizens are unfairly critical of civil servants.

Over the past several years, the president and Congress consistently fail to pass balanced budgets in a timely manner, and in turn, these national leaders blame problems of their own making on federal agencies and their employees. Consequently, the public sees federal employees as a national problem because they are basing their opinions largely on what they are hearing about government workers from politicians and the press, and what they are hearing is mostly not good.

The truth is that federal employees do provide essential and crucial services needed on a daily basis. And these valuable services are provided at a small fraction of the federal budget. According to the written testimony of Congressional Budget Office (CBO) director Douglas Elmendorf, the government spent about $200 billion to compensate federal workers in the fiscal year that ended in September 2011. That's 15 percent of total discretionary spending—the spending levels that lawmakers control through appropriations. In fiscal year 2011, discretionary spending totaled $1.35 trillion, or 40 percent of federal outlays—with much of the money going to the Pentagon and to pay for the wars in Iraq and Afghanistan. The $200 billion estimate includes workers' salaries and benefits such as health care and retirement.

Of the $200 billion, about $80 billion went toward civilian employees of the Defense Department and toward other defense-related activities, according to the CBO. The other $120 billion, less than 10 percent of discretionary spending and less than 4 percent of the federal budget, went to nondefense civilian employees, most of whom work for the departments of Veterans Affairs, Homeland Security, Justice, and the Treasury and at the Internal Revenue Service.

> We're not sure how federal employees became the enemy

And these levels of agency spending in 2011 had fallen to the lowest level since 2002. With the $1.2 trillion in automatic spending cuts instituted by sequestration (covered in more detail in chapter 5), agency spending is projected to lag behind inflation by as much as 16 percent by 2021. This will endanger several big programs, including veterans' health care, according to the CBO.[2]

However, because the preponderance of the message about government workers is negative, the general public does not perceive civil service to be valuable to the nation. Far from being perceived as the national treasure that it is, it has, in fact, become something to be routinely disparaged. Owing to their general lack of awareness of the critical services they receive from the federal government each and every day, the general public is not aware of and does not appreciate these services and their fellow citizens who provide them. *Can't something be done to remedy this situation?* We are going to suggest some solutions to this problem throughout the remainder of this book.

We feel compelled to write this book because federal employees don't have a real voice. There are employee unions, but federal workers don't have one strong, consolidated union to speak for them. As federal employees representing their agencies, they can't lobby Congress, and in this capacity, they can't ask Congress for money, tell them of their budget problems, or tell them of their struggles in attracting and retaining the best and the brightest. Even with these well-established limitations, they are also people with families. They, too, work hard every day because they need to pay their bills. They want to keep their children safe, educate them, and

provide opportunities for them to be successful adults. They have mortgages or rent to pay just like everybody else.

We're not sure how federal employees became the enemy. As the employees in any organization, federal employees are not perfect—there are some who spend the day chitchatting; there are those who spend the day waiting to retire. The federal government is not perfect; however, no group should be labeled by the worst few among it.

Federal Agencies Aren't Assertively Promoting the Vital Work They Do, Causing the Public to Be Uninformed or Misinformed of What Federal Employees Do and Why They Do It

Our government must do a much better job of selling itself and its mission if it is to change the public's perception and attract vital new talent and enthusiasm from prospective hires in the Millennial Generation. Many young people today want to do something meaningful, to make a difference in the world. They show a very high degree of engagement in civic issues. Studies have shown that Millennials are very public service oriented, but today's college graduates are increasingly less frequently including government service in their definition of public service.

The Partnership for Public Service analyzed the results of the 2011 National Association of Colleges and Employers (NACE) Student Survey of 35,401 students from 599 colleges and universities from all fifty states and the District of Columbia. The results are both alarming and replete with challenges for federal hiring managers and human resources professionals who are charged with attracting a new generation of skilled employees to government.

Most startling is the finding that just 6 percent of the college students who were surveyed plan to work in government at the local, state, or federal level, the lowest number expressing an intention to join the public sector (and down more than one-quarter of the interested student base) since 2008, the year the NACE survey first asked the question, when more than 8 percent of the respondents expressed plans to work at the local, state, or federal level.

In 2011, the survey asked for the first time specifically about federal employment aspirations, and only 2.3 percent of respondents reported that they plan to work for the U.S. government.[3] This percentage is likely to decrease. Disillusioned by furloughs, budget cuts, pay freezes, and the 2013 shutdown, Millennials are beginning to sour on government work. This troubling scenario could change tomorrow, but it will change for the better only if the government greatly steps up its marketing and recruiting efforts.

> So who are civil servants, anyway? And why should anyone care?

At this point, it is important to note that we believe there is, indeed, a quite compelling story to tell that strongly supports the value and nobility of federal service. But you may be asking, "So who are civil servants, anyway?" Sure, it seems that most everyone knows that postal workers, Social Security officers, and the IRS are civil servants. But who are the ones most people don't see? And why should anyone care?

To be sure, there certainly is a unique role of the federal government that no one else (state, local, private) can perform. For starters, when there are catastrophic events, people look to federal agencies for relief. Federal agencies can garner resources across jurisdictions by pulling together the appropriate entities and expertise both nationally and internationally. Other entities on their own have limited resources but, individually, have the appropriate skills to make a combined and coordinated response quick and effective. You can recall examples when national responses to emergencies were effective and when they were not. When they were effective, appropriate resources were made readily available. When they were not, more likely it was for a lack of readily available and appropriate resources.

For whom do people look when a national emergency occurs? Well, they expect a fast, efficient, and effective federal government. To prevent catastrophes or ensure quick responses when catastrophes occur, there has to be an organization—strong, professional, and efficient—at the ready. Without strong federal government involvement from federal employees, regular people are left to their own resources without protection, without recourse, and without help in tragic situations.

Or consider how we monitor the health of our economy. Did you know that the federal government produces monthly and quarterly snapshots of key sectors within the U.S. economy? These snapshots are known as economic indicators. They are used by businesses for economic forecasts, market research, and financial decision making. The economic indicators track trends in bellwether industries such as housing construction, trade, and manufacturing. They give us timely and crucial insight into the current health of the U.S. economy. The problem is, though, that the accuracy and timeliness of these indicators are being put at risk by across-the-board budget cuts, staff furloughs, and contracting disruptions. Why does this matter?

It matters because good, reliable, and timely data, free from political influences, on the status of the nation's society and economy are needed by democracies if citizens are to make good, data-driven decisions about whom they elect and how to invest well for today and tomorrow. Without the contributions of civil servants that produce these indicators, our economic and business decision-makers would be flying blind.

Government service offers an extraordinary opportunity to make a difference, to make a tremendous contribution to our country. The need for federal agencies to tell their stories was summed up well in a recent article by Tom Shoop for *Government Executive Magazine.* According to Shoop, agencies are just not very eager to tell their stories. He writes, "Officials, especially political appointees, want to control the message. To them, openness and transparency are all about data sets, finely crafted blog posts and carefully managed social media outreach. They want to strictly regulate what gets said and when. The Obama administration, for example, put a virtual clampdown on releasing information and allowing interviews with key officials in the months leading up to the election." Shoop continues,

> In an online age, agencies are in some ways getting better at telling their own stories. But they're much worse at helping those who want to report on their activities from the outside understand what government is really doing. Indeed, some

media relations offices now seem to take the position that their job is to stand between outsiders and agency officials, providing a barrier to any questions about what's happening inside the walls of government. This, in turn, has bred cynicism among reporters. As a result, the reporting on government over the past decade at least has become almost uniformly negative.

> Whenever Congress fails to approve a comprehensive budget, the government runs the risk of shutting down.

It may be difficult for agencies to get reporters to pay attention to their stories, and to help them understand what's really important. But if government officials don't do that, the only time reporters will pay attention to them is after a scandal erupts. And at that point, you can guarantee your message isn't going to be heard. Just ask the folks at the General Services Administration. Agencies can't stop people outside government from producing stories about what's happening inside it. So, what harm is there in trying to help them do so in an informed way?[4]

Political Leaders—Entrusted to Pass Federal Balanced Budgets, on Time, Allowing Federal Agencies to Work within Reliable and Predictable Fiscal Cycles—Aren't Doing the Jobs They Were Elected to Do

In an article titled "The Making of the Federal Budget" printed in the Fed Page of the *Washington Post* on April 8, 2013, Josh Hicks explains how budgeting for the federal government is a complex and multilayered process that bears little resemblance to Americans' household budgets. The president, by law, is supposed to submit a budget request for the next fiscal year before the first Monday in February, although many administrations have missed this deadline by several weeks. (For example, in 2013, the president's budget was submitted during the second week in April.) Then, the House and Senate develop a series of appropriations bills to come up with unified legislation. After that, the president can sign the reconciliation bill into law, in effect finalizing the budget.

The president and Congress are supposed to finalize a budget by October 1, which is when the government's fiscal year begins. However, this deadline has been consistently missed by the past several administrations. Whenever Congress fails to approve a comprehensive budget, the government runs the risk of shutting down. To prevent this from happening, Congress is forced to adopt short-term spending plans (continuing resolutions) to keep the government operating.

Concerning the issue of the budget gridlock we experienced in 2013, Hicks explains that "part of the issue is that the Senate failed to produce a budget resolution after 2009, when Democrats controlled both chambers of Congress. The House has passed budget resolutions since then, but Democrats have viewed the proposals as unpalatable and a sign that Republicans were not serious about negotiating."[5]

When the president and Congress don't agree, and cannot effectively make needed changes, ask yourself, who has the ultimate power over the federal government? Don't we, as responsible citizens, have a duty to contact our congressional *representatives* to make our needs known? In the interest of holding our leaders, who represent us, accountable, don't we have the right and the duty to vote for representatives that will do their job in an effective and timely manner? Abraham Lincoln once said that "the people of the United States are the rightful masters of both Congress and the Courts, not to overthrow the Constitution, but to overthrow the men who pervert the Constitution."[6] Think about it.

> Is it too much for us to demand that our elected officials do the jobs they were elected by the American people to do?

The ultimate "supervisors" of the federal government are the president and Congress. The president issues directives. Congress determines the federal budget and ultimately sets federal government priorities based on what it provides money to do.

"The Civil Service has no mechanism for reforming itself organically—it has to rely on the President and Congress to initiate major change. Not even a cabinet secretary can overhaul the human resources system in a department without congressional approval. But Congress has paid little attention to the widening gap between demands of increasingly vast and complex government programs and the ability of the government personnel to deliver them."[7]

Elected representatives in Congress determine which rules, standards, and laws the federal government can uphold based on where and how its budget can be spent. Remember the golden rule that whoever has the money makes the rules. But wait, don't we the people have a say? Is it too much for us to demand that our elected officials do the jobs they were elected by the American people to do?

We certainly do need to get our national debt under control. But as part of this attempt, federal pay freezes and job losses seem to be the new normal. In this tight fiscal environment, those serving the federal government certainly do have the responsibility to adapt and to continuously improve performance and productivity. Like workers in the private sector, federal employees also need to incorporate new ways of doing work made possible by the digital age. Of course, they need to continuously make adaptations in their work, their organizational structures, and their working styles. Also, waste still needs to be addressed, as in any business or institution, for the wise use of resources. And for years, indeed, civil servants have been doing so, serving as unsung heroes but being treated like scapegoats.

But as resources continue to be frozen or diminished federal employees simply won't be able to keep doing more, better and faster, with less. At some point, it's going to mean doing less with less. This means there will have to be program cuts, and this will translate into fewer services being provided to the public. All too often, this, in turn, elicits a public outcry and the search for scapegoats.

Individual Citizens Aren't Fulfilling Their Civic Duty—to Be Informed and Engaged in the Conduct of Our Democracy—and This Contributes to Degradation in Federal Services

While people are pointing fingers, they often forget that it was they, themselves who asked Congress to reduce the size of government. There are those who want all government to disappear. All the way back to 1981, President Reagan said about the government related to the economic problems of the day, "In this present crisis, government is not the solution to our problem. Government is the problem."[8]

> Does our nation really want government to go away—even the safety-related institutions that develop standards for education, pay, and health and agencies that sponsor beneficial research for the people?

Both Republican and Democratic leaders alike have used the government and its federal employees, whom they are supposed to supervise and support, as pawns in their political games. You know, it's not too often that you see a top executive for a Fortune 500 company belittling the company mission or its employees. Yet this happens all the time in Washington, and it demoralizes the existing federal workforce and makes it hard to attract the best new employees to the U.S. Civil Service.

Does our nation really want government to go away—even the safety-related institutions that develop standards for education, pay, and health and agencies that sponsor beneficial research for the people? History suggests that this will never happen. Politicians have tried for years to eliminate "the government" but have not been able to complete this task. They have succeeded, however, in making this government more and more ineffective, even in pursuing the basic policies they were created to oversee. So what, then, is government good for now?

While the government aims to protect everyone, in particular, it exists for the protection of regular people—people like you, people like us; people who go day to day earning a living, raising their children, paying their bills, and volunteering in their communities. Regular people can't keep a lawyer on the payroll to protect their interests.

Because most private citizens don't have a payroll, they don't have a congressman or governor or mayor or other state or local representative in their back pocket or even as a close friend. When something happens to them, where do they go for help? They go to the federal government. True, the federal government is not perfect, but it provides essential services every day.

So here's a question: Shouldn't our leadership be working to make it better, not to hamstring or eliminate it? Accountability in a democracy requires knowing who is making decisions regarding the allocation and distribution of public resources. And the voting, tax-paying public should be holding our national leaders accountable to provide good value in service for each tax dollar paid.

Notes to Chapter 1

[1] "The People's Vote: 100 Documents That Shaped America," *U.S. News and World Report,* http://www.usnews.com/usnews/documents/docpages/document_page48.htm.

[2] "Keeping Tabs on the Federal Government," *Washington Post,* October 26, 2011.

[3] Partnership for Public Service, "Federal Leaders Face Challenges Attracting Top College Graduates to Government Service," February 6, 2012.

[4] Tom Shoop, "Tell Your Story," *Government Executive Magazine,* January–February 2013, 4.

[5] Josh Hicks, "The Making of the Federal Budget," *Washington Post,* April 8, 2013, A15.

[6] Excerpt from "Political Debates between Lincoln and Douglas," http://www.bartleby.com/251/pages/page494.html.

[7] Linda J. Bilmes and W. Scott Gould, *The People Factor: Strengthening America by Investing in Public Service* (Washington, D.C.: Brookings Institution Press, 2009).

[8] Mark Holzer, ed., *Public Service: Callings, Commitments, and Contributions* (Oxford: Westview Press, 2000).

Chapter 2
The Making of a Civil Servant

Here is one example of a civil service career that took many turns and jobs changes from nonprofessional to senior professional. The federal government is an excellent place to do this. It is a place where one can create their own path and serve the people of this great nation. I grew up in the District of Columbia but never wanted a government job. I believed it would be boring and also thought the job would not pay competitively when compared to private industry. I was fortunate to have the opportunity to discover the excitement that can be found in government work as I worked for various federal agencies during summers in high school and college.

My federal service began as a summer aide while in high school. Summer aides tended to be assigned the menial tasks that were necessary that full-time employees did not have the time to handle. We didn't mind this at all. Many of us were poor and needed money for clothing and other miscellaneous expenses. Our needs were simple, and there were federal programs that gave poor young people like me the opportunity to earn money over the summer months and provide needed services at minimum wage. We were glad to have jobs, and we were also happy for the sense of responsibility our jobs gave us.

While in college, I moved on to a more intern-type summer employment, although I was not called an intern. I worked for the Department of Labor in the Occupational Safety and Health Administration (OSHA). I don't remember much about my work at

OSHA. I do remember the work of the staff I met there. I still believe that ensuring safe working conditions of men and women across the U.S. is important. I moved on from there to work for the Department of Treasury's Office of the Comptroller of the Currency (OCC) and learned about federal hiring practices which can be rather complex. Individuals working in federal agencies' human resources offices go through numerous job applications every day trying to match the appropriate candidates for the appropriate jobs. This duty is critical but handled mostly behind the scenes. The hired individuals tend to thank the person who hired them and not the one who placed them on the list to get the opportunity to be selected.

Ultimately, I ended up joining the OCC as a full-time fed while I worked on my college education. I found a home in the Office of the National Bank Examiner (ONBE). The folks for whom I worked reviewed and regulated national banks (recall the guy in *It's a Wonderful Life* who inspected the books at the Bailey Building and Loan Association). Almost any bank with "National" in its name came under the scrutiny of the ONBE.

The federal government offers a wealth of opportunities to energetic, hardworking innovators, and my experiences at the OCC proved that to me. I eventually moved on from the OCC, but I look back on this move with some regret on occasion because the OCC was unlike any other agency I have ever served.

I moved on to the Peace Corps where I worked with wonderful people both in the United States and abroad. During this time, total quality management (TQM) or quality control was moving through the federal government with the intent of process improvement. References regarding this term and its history can be found in the Bibliography section of this book. Contractors came in and taught us how to work better together and how to streamline work processes. This was the first of my many experiences with process improvement, morale building, workplace efficiency; learn your personality and leadership training in the federal government. If you don't know yourself when you join civil service, stay with it and you will.

I eventually joined the Department of Transportation (DOT), where I stayed for the remainder of my federal career. I believe that DOT is an important organization for America. The DOT makes a fascinating study into the less-known workings of the federal government. If you don't understand the federal government, pick a department other than the Department of Defense and study it.

The federal government is much more than politicians, war and taxes. It also safeguards health and wellness, food, education, roads, bridges, parks, and oceans. The federal government develops and enforces food safety standards. It develops standards for water and air quality. It responds to emergencies across the U.S. and the world. The list can go on and on. After the 2013 government shutdown, many more personally know what the federal government does to support the people across this great nation.

I recommend DOT as a great place to work for anyone who wishes to improve the standard of living of regular people and at the same time experience a variety of challenges to improve personal wisdom and critical thinking. I met many people during my years at DOT and held various positions with increasing leadership and other responsibilities, for example, budget preparation.

Preparing the budget for an agency is challenging. All agencies have to prepare a budget for each fiscal year by a date certain. This is a lot of work and requires much coordination among different offices. It's even more challenging when the budget you spend so much time preparing is just left to sit year after year. Still budgets get written and sent off for approval on time every year.

Most people I dealt with wanted to do excellent work, but the resources to do their jobs well became more and more scarce. Offices began competing for the limited resources which lead to increasing tensions among staff and across offices within organizations. We believed our work was important but there was not enough money to go around for all. It became something of a tossup as to which projects survived and which did not.

> As I celebrate many years in the federal government, there remains a cloud hanging over civil service. The work of civil servants everywhere is just as critical to this nation as the work of anyone else.

In 2013, the government remains in the spotlight as a national problem. According to John Donahue in his 2008 book *The Warping of Government Work,* somewhere in U.S. history, "a gap opened between the world of work in the government and in the rest of the U.S. economy. I am convinced, though, that the federal government is critical to protecting the individual rights of all Americans. Its role is also to support the people in times of national and international emergency.

We are a nation that promotes rights and freedoms, and such rights and freedoms are not automatic. Individual private entities will tend to protect their own interests. We therefore need a national entity to protect the rights and freedoms of the people, and that's where the government comes in.

The segregation of the public and private working worlds has been incremental, largely accidental, and like other gradual transformations less noticed hence less understood than the consequences warrant."[1] Some might agree with this statement still now in 2013, "All too often American government is not smart enough (because private alternatives drain away the best personnel) and not supple enough (because workers sheltering in government's middle class bastion quite rationally resist change)."[2]

I am now a retiree and very proud of my service to the federal government and the American people. As I celebrate many years in the federal government, there remains a cloud hanging over civil service. The work of civil servants everywhere is just as critical to this nation as the work of anyone else. One American worker is not more important than another. Civil service is work to be honored. It takes a special individual to be a civil servant.

I was able to help bring on experienced people and ready to work young people to federal service. They were full of energy and high ideals and wanted to accomplish much for their new offices and organization. I hope I did not bring them in under false pretenses.

These new hires want to affect change, make government work better and improve the nation. They cannot accomplish this without the appropriate resources and the support of their ultimate leaders, Congress and the White House.

I have seen many good projects get started and die due to lack of resources. We were asked why, what happened. We could not say that "you did not give us enough money to get it done" to our leadership.

Ultimately I consider myself extremely fortunate. I had the opportunity to rise from a clerk typist to a senior manager. Now I understand that I stayed on this civil service ride and voluntarily managed people and budgets and I believe I made a difference.

Notes to Chapter 2

[1] John D. Donahue, *The Warping of Government Work* (Cambridge, Mass.: Harvard University Press, 2008), 5.
[2] Ibid, 141.

Chapter 3
The Road to the Senior Executive Service

I graduated from a small, private Midwestern university in 1976 with a Bachelor of Science degree in business administration. I probably would have looked for a job in the Chicago area were it not for the fact that I was engaged to be married in two months and my fiancée was going to college for one more year in the Washington, D.C., area. So, before graduating, I looked for a job near the capital. I landed a position as a grade 7 survey statistician at the U.S. Census Bureau in Suitland, Maryland, just outside the District. I considered this to be a big break. I wanted to work for the government because I thought it was a good place in which I could make a difference, and, perhaps, in which I could rise to a top position within my particular agency.

I began work on the Census of Retail Trade (part of the Economic Census taken every five years) and was always looking for more work to do. I found myself in many challenging assignments. Before the age of thirty, I was already in charge of the branch into which I was first hired, the Retail Census Branch (comprising about ten professional and clerical staff members). By working hard and learning something new every day, I had gained extensive knowledge of all phases of economic census taking, including questionnaire design, response micro-record editing, summary level macro-record analysis, and dissemination of final results.

It was sometime around the late 1980s, when I had been serving as branch chief for a few years, that I began to realize that I had some important decisions to make with respect to the next phase of my career. I was working hard every day and greatly enjoyed what I was doing. As branch chief, I was heavily involved in recruiting new employees, and in training and developing them, and had begun to develop an extensive network of public and private contacts. At that point, I had to decide whether to try to go higher in the organization. How high did I want to shoot? Why would I want to do that? Would it be for the money, or for the opportunity to be able to do more? As my wife and I had two young daughters, what would be the effect on my family?

As I thought through all these questions and issues, what it finally boiled down to was that I felt obligated to use the gifts God had given me to do the best I could for the most people and that I would be able to do that only if I were in a higher leadership position. Living by the adage "to whom much is given much is expected," I felt like it was my duty to do my best to commit my talents to improving the workplace and the work and the products we produced.

As quality guru W. Edwards Deming (himself a former Census Bureau employee) once said, "The aim of leadership should be to improve the performance of man and machine, to improve quality, to improve output, and simultaneously to bring pride of workmanship to people ... The leader also has responsibility to improve the system – i.e., to make it possible, on a continuing basis, for everybody to do a better job with greater satisfaction."[1] Ultimately I wanted to be in a leadership position having enough leverage to create a work environment that was productive and, to the greatest extent, enjoyable. I realized I was going to have to go higher to have that degree of influence.

So, after seven years as chief of the Retail Census Branch, I successfully competed for a higher position and was promoted to assistant division chief, heading four branches with about seventy employees and responsible for the collection, analysis, and release of the monthly and annual surveys of retail trade and wholesale trade. This was a major change from the work on the five-year economic census and involved producing principal economic indicators that moved the stock market after they were released (like the Advance Monthly Retail Sales Report released just nine working days after the data month covered).

In this position, I believe I was instrumental in introducing modernized automated survey taking to the major surveys in my division, replacing pencil-and-paper techniques. By 1994, after four years of success at this level of management, I was ready to start looking to move again to the next level—the Senior Executive Service (SES), where I could make a big difference, with more and more opportunities to serve the public.

The SES was established in 1978 and implemented in 1979 as a separate personnel system, covering most of the top managerial and policy positions in the federal government. The idea was for the SES to provide greater authority to agencies in attracting, managing, and retaining executive resources. This became a system in which outstanding performers were rewarded and executives were held accountable for individual and organizational performance. That meant there might not be bonuses some years, and your pay might even get docked by 10 percent if you were not doing a good job. Much emphasis was placed on competence, dedication, and accountability. Most positions required substantial professional and/or specific program expertise.

I was only forty, and I was looking to go higher. I had decided to really try to serve the nation in a greater way, but at the same time, I would be putting my reputation on the line. The pay was fairly good (pay compression had been dealt with to a somewhat adequate degree back then), but in my mind, the opportunity to serve was an even greater incentive.

> Although it is true, in many important ways, that I did pay, personally, for my professional success, in the final analysis, I believe I served my country with integrity and commitment

The problem was that there were, and are, only a little more than seven thousand positions available across the country, and nationwide competition at this level was quite keen. But I went ahead and competed for an SES position at the Census Bureau in 1994—I swung and I missed. I actually applied for SES positions several more times before I finally succeeded: for a different position in 1994; for another one in 1997; and for yet another one in 2000.

I had four pitches and four strikes, but at least the last two strikes were loud, long, just-missed-the-home-run foul balls, so I had not yet struck out and was getting closer to first base. I finally reached the SES in July 2001 as chief of the Service Sector Statistics Division. Although I had moved to a different division along the way, I was actually coming back to my home division, the one in which I started my career. The number of employees in the division had gone from about 175 to 250 over time, and the division now boasted a much higher ratio of professional to clerical employees compared to its composition in the 1970s. This division was a good place for me to take charge and make improvements. And I knew I was taking on a very big job and was excited about it.

So I reached the ranks of the SES before the age of fifty and still had a bit of gas left in the tank to try to make a difference. With the aid of the excellent staff I inherited and eventually built into an even stronger workforce, we really did make a significant difference. We launched several new service statistics programs to better measure the U.S. economy, including the first economic indicator introduced by the federal government in more than thirty years.

With an emphasis on putting data users and the tax-paying public first, we also introduced new ways of accessing economic indicator data on the web and via the America's Economy mobile app, the first mobile app developed by the Census Bureau. We created a better awareness of these important data and increased the value and accessibility of these market-moving numbers to hundreds of thousands of data users in our nation and across the world. I was instrumental in getting these programs initiated and implemented in large part because of the influential leadership role I had as a member of the SES.

Although it is true, in many important ways, that I did pay, personally, for my professional success, in the final analysis, I believe I served my country with integrity and commitment, and I do not regret my career decision to go higher and eventually to work in the ranks of the SES. However, as we cover in subsequent chapters, today it seems that fewer people are making that decision.

Ultimately, the attitude among some in the political ruling components of government demonstrates a lack of appreciation for the value of a civil service career in general and federal SES leadership in particular. And all of this is part of the larger problem, addressed by this book, which is a general devaluing of what the federal government means to the citizens it serves.

At the same time, of course, U.S. taxpayers are and should be demanding the best value of service possible for their tax dollars. People should, and do, expect more from government organizations than from private organizations for the reason that their hard-earned money is what is funding the government. And, as we will talk about in Chapter 4, civil servants do many things that the public cares deeply about on a daily basis.

With that in mind, a few final questions are (1) What can federal departments and their respective agencies do to raise awareness of what they do and why they do it? (2) What can our national political leaders do to be part of the solution and not part of the problem? (3) What can all of us, as the general citizenry, do to hold our political leaders accountable? and (4) How can we make civil service careers attractive for prospective hires from the entry level all the way up through to the SES? We will address these questions in Chapter 6.

Note to Chapter 3

W. Edwards Deming, *Out of the Crisis* (Cambridge, Mass.: MIT Press, 1986), 248-249.

PART II

RESTORING HONOR TO U.S. CIVIL SERVICE

Chapter 4
The Many Services Civil Service Workers Provide

> What our elected leaders have taken from us is not money but our trust, faith and confidence. In my mind, this is far worse than a temporary loss of pay.
>
> —Mike Penland, retired US. Air Force officer

Civil service employees do not receive much recognition for their work. There are no parades for civil servants. Although many aren't looking for recognition, federal workers would still like to be appreciated, for what they do.

The impartial, nonpartisan nature of the U.S. Civil Service—comprising a professional, dedicated civilian workforce—is one of the hallmarks of the United States. As you look at what is going on in countries around the world, our country is the exception, not the rule, in this respect. As U.S. citizens, we should be thankful for what we have and do what is in our power to keep the dedicated civil service workforce from slipping away.

> "Civil service workers serve in the background of our lives every day. Because they are in the background, they tend to be forgotten, overlooked, and misunderstood"

Although there are those who denigrate federal service and work tirelessly to eliminate the federal government, there are, thankfully, those today who still celebrate federal service and recognize the work of dedicated civil servants. The Samuel J. Heyman Service to America medals[1] are awarded annually to celebrate excellence in federal civil service. These medals are presented by a nonprofit, nonpartisan Partnership for Public Service. The awardees are recognized as outstanding federal employees whose important, behind-the-scenes work is advancing the health, safety, and well-being of Americans.

The 2013 national sponsors included Booz Allen Hamilton, the Boston Consulting Group, and United Technologies. There are various other sponsors at different levels. One career achievement finalist for 2013 "pioneered models to better forecast the path and intensity of hurricanes during the past three decades to help communities and first responders prepare for the severe storms, saving countless lives, homes and businesses."[2]

Research is a critical area and as such is where the federal government has sponsored or contributed to groundbreaking scientific results. "Today, researchers are likely to be funded by a mix of grants from various government agencies, institutions, and foundations. For example, a 2007 study of the movement of carbon in the ocean was funded by the National Science Foundation, the U.S. Department of Energy, the Australian Cooperative Research Centre, and the Australian Antarctic Division."[3]

Science is paid for with both federal and private funds. This strikes a balance to ensure a lack of bias in reported research results, particularly in those studies that impact the life, health, and safety of all of us. We, the federal tax payers, contribute to such critical and necessary work. Private enterprises are not always guaranteed to conduct and report results of scientific studies that may detrimentally impact their financial well-being.

The federal government is an impartial entity that can and does, in general, serve as an unbiased researcher. For example, the National Cancer Institute (NCI), part of the National Institutes of Health and the Department of Health and Human Services, is the nation's principal agency for cancer research and coordinates the National Cancer Program. The NCI receives its funding from Congress. The cancer research program coordinated by NCI investigates the causes, prevention, detection, diagnosis, and treatment of cancer through various research projects and clinical trials.[4]

> The past several years, federal workers have taken on more and more responsibilities as their colleagues have retired and are not replaced.

In addition to conducting and sponsoring critical research, federal workers are deployed to areas of natural disaster throughout the nation and the world. In response to the East Coast floods of 2013, federal workers traveled to affected areas to support clean-up and repair efforts and to call in other national, international, state, local, and private resources, where necessary.

Many federal employees have volunteered to put themselves in harm's way in such places as Iraq and Afghanistan in support of the administrative needs of the deployed troops and the people who live in these regions of the world. Secretaries of various federal departments send out calls for volunteers for such work, and civil servants leave their homes and families to serve where they are needed.

Many already know about the federal workers who monitor and inspect the many U.S. roads and bridges. We also know of the federal workers who ensure the safe movement of trucks and long-distance buses on our roads and highways. We certainly know of and appreciate those federal workers who ensure the safe transport of people in the air and on the water.

In addition to these civil servants, there are those federal workers who inspect buildings where we work and learn, single and multifamily housing where we live, and playgrounds where our children play to ensure that these facilities are environmentally sound, safe, and up to national standards for those with special needs. Such buildings can be hazardous to walk through. They can also be located in dangerous neighborhoods. There are civil servants who do this job daily because they believe this work is important and necessary.

Data and information are also critical for the economic well-being of our nation. Federal agencies collect data on where we live and work, what we buy, how we move about the nation, where we travel both internationally and domestically, and numerous other factors that allow for the appropriate investment of limited resources in all communities around the United States. Without such statistics, we would not know where to build a road, where to repair a bridge, or where to build and maintain public transportation. Without this information, businesses could not plan their short-

and long-term investments, and new businesses could not strategically form and grow. Data and information are not noticed in general as necessary until some private individual, organization, or interest group has some critical data need. Then questions and complaints arise about why such information does not exist.

We already know that civil servants fight fires, rescue those in danger, and conduct interdictions to keep illegal drugs out of the hands of our children. We also know that civil servants test and evaluate the air we breathe, the food we eat, and the water we drink. Civil service workers serve in the background of our lives every day. Because they are in the background, they tend to be forgotten, overlooked, and misunderstood. We encourage you to take a look at the Appendix of this book, which contains a list of websites providing information about U.S. government departments and agencies.

Retiring Civil Servants Are Taking Knowledge, Skills, and Expertise Out of the Federal Government in Record Numbers

According to the *Washington Post,* 66,600 federal workers retired in the first ten months of fiscal year 2013.[5] There are thousands more in every federal agency who are or will be eligible for retirement soon. Most agencies are at or nearly at 30 percent of their workforce that will be eligible to retire by 2016. Federal agencies are not replacing workers by choice or cannot replace these workers in similar numbers due to budget constraints or general plans to reduce the numbers of employees. This "downsizing" is not new.

Over the past several years, federal workers have taken on more and more responsibilities as their colleagues have retired and are not replaced. Some in Congress and the general public are applauding this reduction in the federal workforce. Some even joke about it. Some comments in the *Washington Post* article referenced above, actually celebrate this disturbing and nearly silent trend.

Many are unaware of the true contributions of these long time federal workers. Problems occur as expert employees leave by the thousands. There are those who are leaving with critical expertise that will be difficult, if not impossible, to replace.

The Office of Personnel Management provides statistics on the characteristics of the federal workforce. The following information comes from a September 30, 2012, report.[6]

> **Age:** 47.0 years average for non-seasonal, full-time permanent employees
> **Length of Service:** 13.7 years average for full-time permanent employees
> **Retirement Eligibility:** 67% of full-time permanents covered under Civil Service Retirement (excluding hires since January 1984)
> **Education Level:** 48.1% have Bachelor's Degree or higher degree
> **Gender:** 56.4% men and 43.6% women
> **Race and National Origin:** 34% minority group members: 17.7% Black, 8.0% Hispanic, 5.8% Asian, .409% Native Hawaiian/Other Pacific Islander, 2.1% Native American
> **Disability Status:** 7.9% have disabilities
> **Veterans Preference:** 24.46% have

veterans' preference (5.02% are Vietnam Era veterans)
Retired Military: 7.7% of total: 1.7% officers and 6.0% enlisted personnel

As can be seen from these statistics, if federal employees are not replaced in significant numbers as they retire over the next few years, the civilian workforce could be severely depleted.

Notes to Chapter 4

[1] Samuel J. Heyman Service to America Medals, "Celebrating Accomplishments of America's Public Services," available at: http://servicetoamericamedals.org/SAM/index.shtml as of August 8, 2013.

[2] Ibid.

[3] "Who Pays for Science?" Understanding Science: How Science Really Works, http://undsci.berkeley.edu/article/who_pays.

[4] National Cancer Institute, "Cancer Research Funding," NCI Factsheet, http://www.cancer.gov/cancertopics/factsheet/NCI/research-funding.

[5] Darla Cameron and Cristina Rivero, "Wave of Federal Retirement," *Washington Post*, August 26, 2013, http://www.washingtonpost.com/wp-srv/special/politics/federal-retirements/.

[6] Office of Personnel Management, Profile of Federal Civilian Non-Seasonal Full-Time Employees." Data, Analysis and Documentation, Federal Employment Reports, http://www.opm.gov/policy-data-oversight/data-analysis-documentation/federal-employment-reports/reports-publications/profile-of-federal-civilian-non-postal-employees

Chapter 5
The Challenges of Civil Service Today

> The Federal government employs one of the most skilled and diverse workforces in the world. We can't continue to pursue policies that undermine their livelihoods. The surest path to a second-rate Federal workforce is to keep doing exactly what we're doing today.
>
> —William R. Dougan, President, National Federation of Federal Employees

The U.S. Civil Service actually is a great place to work and serve! It employs people from diverse backgrounds for the purpose of serving the public. Civil servants support the safety, security, prosperity, and overall well-being of our nation. Through their service, they make this nation a better and safer place to live. They make a difference.

Civil servants need to be valued and paid their worth. This is important for existing workers and to attract new workers from the upcoming generations. The problem is that civil servants are no longer honored, because, as we stated in chapter 1,

- Federal agencies don't assertively promote the vital work they do, causing the public to be uninformed, or misinformed, about what federal employees do and why they do it.
- Political leaders—entrusted with passing balanced budgets, on time, allowing federal agencies to work within reliable and

predictable fiscal cycles—aren't doing the jobs they were elected to do.
- Individual citizens aren't fulfilling their civic duty to be informed and engaged in the conduct of our democracy.

There are several symptoms resulting from this main problem and its causes. This chapter describes these resulting symptoms. Chapter 6 then suggests potential remedies—in the form of calls to action for government agencies, for prospective hires who might be considering working for the federal government, and for the general public—that might put us on a path to restore the honor of the U.S. Civil Service today and tomorrow.

Federal Work Is No Longer Honored: What Are the Resulting Symptoms?

The Work Life of the Civil Servant Today Is Challenging, and Civil Servants Feel Under-appreciated

Most government agencies, especially non-defense, non-security agencies in the executive branch, have been dealing with serious ongoing budget constraints since at least the time of zero-based budgeting in the latter half of the 1970s. Thirty years of budget constraints have taken a tremendous toll on agency management resources in all administrative areas (human resources, accounting, contract management, budget and finance) as agencies have attempted to reduce indirect program support in favor of program funding.

In addition, agencies have also had to adhere to

congressional action (such as the Gramm–Rudman–Hollings spending controls and reductions of the 1980s) and the assorted management improvement efforts of various administrations, such as the contracting initiatives (read reductions in federal employees) of the Clinton and Bush administrations.[1]

Then, in March 2013, after Congress failed to reach an agreement on an alternative deficit-reduction deal, automatic, across-the-board federal budget cuts known as the sequester went into effect all over government. Sequestration kicked in on March 1, 2013, and was the result of Congress' failure to trim the deficit by $1.2 trillion over a decade. And, of course, there was the partial government shutdown in October 2013.

Federal agency budgets will be cut by $85 billion by the end of 2013, with the total split between the Defense Department and the rest of the federal government. Additional cuts will come in future years as long as the sequester remains in effect. Many agencies are prepared to furlough employees one day each week, meaning pay cuts for those employees and diminished services for everyone. More than a million federal workers face unpaid leave.

At the Pentagon alone, almost eight hundred thousand of its workers are at risk of losing up to 20 percent of their pay through furloughs. In April 2013, people were complaining as furloughs of Federal Aviation Administration employees affected their air travel experience. These complaints were immediately addressed by Congress and the president. What happens to the rest of the civil servants?

In the wake of these events, the Federal

Workers Alliance, a coalition of twenty unions that represent federal employees, launched an online message board on which workers could post their reactions to the furloughs. Here's one typical post: "30 years ago I swore an oath of office as a federal employee. And for 30 years I have upheld that oath. I agreed to lower than industry wages for years . . . I have even endured the recent lack of cost-of-living increases and the disappearance of 'bonuses' for going above and beyond; I am at the end of my rope. This is going to HURT! And I may even end up losing my house. Really? This is what 30 years of service brought me?"

Or, here is a response to the *Washington Post* Federal Diary columns about the coming furloughs:

> I'm a Federal attorney and the loss of income will most certainly impact me, but I admit it will be easier for me to bear than those who are paid less than I. As these furloughs approach, I begin to worry about how I am going to get the work done. My calendar is full each and every day with meetings, deadlines for documents in court, phone calls to return, emails to answer, questions to clarify and answers to explain, reviews to be done, and trials to conduct. I work through lunch, barely have time to run to the restroom once a day. . . . We've been doing "more with less" for so long, I am pretty sure we can't do "something with nothing." It's easy for the private sector to say that we're overpaid and lazy. It allows them to stop any further examination of what is going on.[2]

It's Challenging for Federal Agencies to Attract and Retain Quality Employees

For our government to succeed, it will continue to need talented, committed, well-trained public servants—across the country and at all levels of government. Various studies have examined factors that influence individuals' decisions to enter public service. A consistent set of themes emerged that identify issues the government must address if it seeks to attract "the best" of any age.

A Council for Excellence in Government survey of distinguished former federal employees cited the following factors as compelling draws to public service:[3]

- Strong sense of mission
- Ability to make a difference in people's lives
- Ability to contribute to the greater good
- Scope and challenges of the work beyond anything available in the private sector
- Opportunity to take on risky tasks that cannot be done by the private sector
- Cutting-edge and ahead-of-the-curve tasks and responsibilities
- Opportunities for increased responsibility and rapid career advancement
- Unusual opportunities to broaden personal knowledge and self-awareness
- Creativity and dedication of coworkers
- Opportunities for women and minorities

However, these factors that attract citizens to public service are strongly countered by the grim realities of the present budget situation. Consider the testimony of James Clapper, director of national intelligence, in a Senate Committee hearing in March 2013 that cuts now may bring unexpected dangers later because sequester budget cuts mean the country is "accepting greater risks." Consider, for example, like other agencies, recruiting by the intelligence community could be hurt by the budget cuts.

"When recruiters court a bright college prospect, they can stress the 'very important, crucial work' of intelligence employees," Clapper said. But he added that recruiters also will have to tell prospects to "bear in mind your pay is going to be capped, and you're subject to whimsical furloughs.... How attractive do you think that's going to be over time?" he asked.

> "I don't know if we succeeded in beating back those small-hearted people who somehow feel it is appropriate to denigrate public service. I don't know what sort of smallness of mind or heart motivates them, but they need to understand that public service matters."

To be sure, civil servants are loyal and dedicated, even in the face of furloughs and budget cuts. But they need to be treated better, because they deserve it. And, for the sake of the up-and-coming generation – our future! – our leaders must take steps to strengthen government, not weaken it.

In response to proposed cuts to federal retirement benefits in the president's 2014 budget plan released in April 2013, federal employees would pay an additional 1.2 percentage points of their pay spread out over three years—0.4 percent annually. J. David Cox Sr., national president of the American Federation of Government Employees, called the retirement proposals a "betrayal" by the administration in the wake of an already enacted increase in salary contributions toward retirement, the salary rate freeze, and sequestration cuts that will force unpaid furloughs. Furthermore, he stated, "The administration seems determined to contribute to a worsening of living standards for federal workers, disabled veterans, and the elderly."[4]

In addition, National Treasury Employees Union president Colleen M. Kelley stated that "Federal employees chose to serve our country through public service but they did not sign up to single-handedly offset a budget deficit they did not cause.

While some administration officials are donating back some of their salary in solidarity with Federal employees, it seems to me that a better approach would be to recognize the value of Federal employees, understand that they have given enough from their own pockets, and not ask them to give any more." She continued, "Federal workers . . . are facing an actual pay cut this year from unpaid furlough days generated by sequestration, on top of the existing pay freeze."[5] And, we might add, federal employees actually contribute to their own salaries through federal and state income tax—they are taxpayers, too!

As John Berry, director of the U.S. Office of Personnel Management (OPM), left his term-limited post in April 2013 in preparation for his next job as ambassador to Australia, he had one big frustration. His parting remarks included, "I don't know if we succeeded in beating back those small-hearted people who somehow feel it is appropriate to denigrate public service. I don't know what sort of smallness of mind or heart motivates them, but they need to understand that public service matters. And these jobs are just too important to not be able to recruit the best and the brightest to do them. . . . Do you want Homer Simpson researching cancer for your children's diseases?" He continued, "You can't freeze pay forever and pretend we are going to be competitive with the Fortune 500. This battle [to increase appreciation for Federal workers] continues. I hope we have laid down some markers. . . . It's just so important."[6]

Earlier, at a meeting with members of the National Council on Federal Labor-Management Relations in March 2013, as reported by the *Federal Times,* Berry had stated that

> 85 percent of our workforce is outside of Washington. The workforce today is the same size it was when Lyndon Johnson was president, and yet we have 60 million more Americans. Don't talk to me about efficiency. Only in this town can the [Government Accountability] Office drag me over the coals on skill gaps and the fact that we cannot hire people to fight cyber security in this nation, and the president in the State of the Union message makes clear that we are facing essentially a pre-9/11 situation with cyber security, and we can't hire people—and yet the next day [we] have the Congress adopt the third year of a pay freeze. And no one sees a connection between these two points. Only in Washington.
>
> I don't know what straw breaks the

camel's back, but I can tell you this: We are close to the edge of the cliff. And all public policy officials, whether they be Republican or Democrat, need to be exercising extreme caution.

We cannot recruit and retain a qualified workforce by freezing their pay forever. We cannot do it by changing their retirement plan on an annual basis. We cannot do it by denigrating public service.[7]

Federal government employment levels through the years including the U.S. Postal Service)

	Executive branch civilians	Total U.S. population	Executive branch employees per 1,000 population
1962 (Kennedy)	2.48 million	186.5 million	13.3
1964 (Johnson)	2.47 million	191.8 million	12.9
1970 (Nixon)	2.94 million[a]	205.0 million	14.4
1975 (Ford)	2.84 million	215.9 million	13.2
1978 (Carter)	2.87 million	222.5 million	12.9
1982 (Reagan)	2.77 million	232.1 million	11.9
1990 (Bush)	3.06 million[a]	249.6 million	12.3
1994 (Clinton)	2.90 million	263.1 million	11.1
2002 (Bush)	2.63 million	287.8 million	9.1
2010 (Obama)	2.65 million[b]	310.3 million[b]	8.4[b]

[a]Figure includes temporary Census Bureau workers. [b]Estimates by OMB and U.S. Census Bureau.
Source: Office of Management and Budget.

As can be seen from the preceding table, the number of federal executive branch civilian employees as a percentage of the U.S. population total has steadily decreased over time. In fact, over the last fifty years, the federal workforce has become much more efficient. With the increase in U.S. population, this means that we have gone from 1 federal employee for every 75 Americans in 1962 to 1 employee per 117 Americans in 2010.

The number of executive branch civilian employees has continued to steadily decrease since 2010. Two hundred twenty thousand federal employees left the federal government in 2012—more than 10 percent of the total workforce.[8]

Baby boomers actually began leaving the federal government in 2005, but the financial crisis and Great Recession that occurred from 2007 to 2009 kept many more from leaving. Retirements from the executive branch were at a low point in 2009, but as the economy has slowly recovered, they have been steadily increasing since then. According to the OPM, retirements are on track to exceed eighty thousand in 2013, the largest federal employee exodus in at least two decades.

And yet, despite the obvious hemorrhaging of federal jobs in recent years, certain members of Congress continue to call for even greater job cuts. In the House-passed FY2014 budget, the plan calls for eliminating two hundred thousand federal jobs through attrition over the next several years. Were this or one of many other similar proposals to actually become law, the federal brain drain would accelerate into overdrive.

The Public Is Unfairly Critical of Federal Employees and Doesn't Recognize the Value of the Civil Services They Receive

As concerned citizens, we all need to become aware of what is going on and, if blame is to be assigned, to make sure the blame is put on the right groups. Here is our take on what is happening today and how it is hurting federal agencies and federal workers.

As Joe Davidson stated in his *Washington Post* Federal Diary column on
June 14, 2013,

> Uncle Sam's reputation has taken a beating lately, and it's his staff that will feel the pain. The recent spate of controversies—revelations about the massive collection of electronic data by the National Security Agency, the Internal Revenue Service's political targeting and conference scandals, and the seizure of Associated Press telephone records—undermines confidence in government. That can't be good for those who make the government work. The sad thing is these scandals represent only a small part of what government does. But they are high-profile items that can adversely shape public opinion. With budget cuts and furloughs, the job of federal employees is tough enough without the added burden these issues bring.[9]

In recent months, reports of average federal salaries being higher than those in private industry have come into the public spotlight.[10] However, using an average pay amount for all federal workers is a mistake. The federal pay scale is so wide from the lowest to the highest that an average is rendered meaningless. True comparison of federal salaries to those in private industry would be accurate and much more appropriate at the job or work level or at the low, medium, and upper income ranges with the number of employees at each of these levels.

Pay studies have shown that federal workers in jobs requiring lower levels of education do have higher compensation than their private sector counterparts, but federal employees in professional and managerial roles earn *less* than they could in the private sector. Artificial ceilings on federal sector pay have made it more difficult for agencies to compete for employees with higher skill levels.

For many years, the large majority of federal employees in the professional ranks have been paid less and less, yet they still have tried to get the same amount of work done. However, it is just human nature for people to react emotionally to the way they are treated, and that ultimately affects performance. The OPM's most recent Federal Employee Viewpoint Survey confirmed a decline in morale and in active engagement in work. Responses were down two percentage points when recommending an organization as a good place to work (67 percent) and three percentage points in satisfaction with jobs (68 percent) and organizations (59 percent).[11]

In a recent interview with the *Washington Post,* Erica L. Groshen, Bureau of Labor Statistics (BLS) commissioner since January 2013 and a former vice president of the Research and Statistics Group at the Federal Reserve Bank of New York, said that the sequestration is affecting the BLS "big time." She said,
> "My first day on the job I had to review the agency sequester plans. BLS is a production operation and the public depends on our data. We can't just say that we won't put out June's unemployment rate, for example.

> We produce many long-term data series with very short turnaround, but the main thing we have done according to our sequestration plan is eliminate three programs: Measuring Green Jobs, International Labor Comparisons and Mass Layoff Statistics. We are also delaying maintenance, postponing training, and slowing down needed improvements. Although we think we've protected our remaining products enough, the belt tightening will affect the quality of our outputs. We just don't know how much yet. . . . We're working very hard to do more with less, but if funding continues at the present level, we will certainly have to cut more programs." [12]

So now, even with pay freezes and furloughs, dedicated government performers keep trying to get the same amount of work done in less time. Why do they do this? And how do they do this?

We think that the answer has to do with the upstanding character of the federal worker. Top-notch workers will continue to perform quite admirably, even under duress. A great example of this kind of dedication was apparent during the "snowpacalypse" of February 2010.

Even with the federal government closed for four days in the second week of that month, federal economic indicators, relied upon by economic decision makers all across the country and the world, continued to be released on schedule. This was due to staff taking on personal hardships and braving virtually impossible travel conditions to come in to the office to get the work done as scheduled.

But the sequestration in 2013 seems like a direct assault on the federal ranks. By taking efficiency measures such as freezing hiring, cutting back on training and travel, and, in many cases, furloughing their employees one day a week, federal agencies and their employees are doing more with less, but they are still doing the job. The economic reports are still being disseminated to the public on time, every time. Warships are still being deployed overseas (although the U.S. Navy recently has had to trim the number of ships it deployed). But there are indications that toward the end of 2013, there are indications that the sequestration will become too much, and it has been going on for too long.

Agencies charged with making our nation more safe, secure, and informed will not be able to keep doing everything they were doing before indefinitely into the future. Indeed, there are signs that even the best performers are becoming discouraged. It is important to note that the federal government cannot afford to lose its best performers, especially at a time when it has become difficult to retain new hires.

There are great costs when high performers resign—productivity suffers, supervisors and others spend extra time with replacements, and customer satisfaction declines. As a result, steps need to be taken now, more than ever before, to retain top-notch workers in the ranks of the U.S. Civil Service. Departments and agencies also need to implement progressive training strategies to ensure that they continue to retain the best and the brightest. To these ends, federal agencies certainly need to offer salaries and benefits to federal employees that remain competitive with the private sector.

In the aforementioned June 14, 2013, Federal

Diary article, a variety of federal employees and others offered their take on how the recent government controversies and scandals were affecting the public's perception of the workforce and workers' morale. Carol Bonosaro, president of the Senior Executives Association, stated, "I have little doubt that the public's perception has already been affected negatively. The public holds a low opinion of Congress and government generally, but now career employees have a big target on their backs."[13]

Joseph Beaudoin, president of the National Active and Retired Federal Employees Association, said, "At the end of the day, Americans' perceptions of our Federal workforce should be shaped by the services Federal workers perform for us all—keeping our food safe, maintaining our communications networks, protecting our national parks, and so much more. The millions of daily Federal employee accomplishments should not—and ultimately will not—be tarnished by the news cycle."[14] And Max Stier, president and chief executive of the Partnership for Public Service, offered, "I am very worried about the health of our workforce.

This is a moment which requires courageous leadership from President Obama and Congress. The public is being given real reason for disappointment with our government, but we will get worse, not better, outcomes if the leadership response is to continue to penalize the entire workforce for the mistakes of a few. We need forthright and targeted handling of the mistakes and improved leadership attention to the needs of the workforce."[15]

Seeing Mostly Negative Issues, Many Prospective Hires May Not See a Civil Service Career as a Worthy Calling

Seeing mostly negative circumstances surrounding federal employment, there is a great danger that prospective hires may not see the civil service as a worthy calling.[16] If they are like most people, they probably do not understand the mission and initiatives of federal agencies. Consequently, they may not see that there are many worthy challenges that the country currently faces that they could help meet. Unfortunately, they may be seeing only the negative challenges and not the opportunities, rewards, and benefits of federal employment. Therefore they may miss out on the many rewarding opportunities that are available today to serve our nation.

Notes to Chapter 5

[1] Woodrow Wilson School Task Force, *The Changing Nature of Government Service,* Final Report, April 13, 2009.

[2] Joe Davidson, "Employees React Ahead of the Sequester," *Washington Post*, February 26, 2013.

[3] Council for Excellence in Government, "Attracting and Keeping the Best and the Brightest: An Online Survey of Council Principals,". Council for Excellence in Government, July 2002.

[4] Joe Davidson, "Give and Take for Federal Workers," *Washington Post*, April 11, 2013.

[5] Ibid.

[6] Joe Davidson, "John Berry Leaves Office of Personnel Management," *Washington Post*, April 10, 2013.

[7] Stephen Losey, "OPM's Berry: 'We are close to the edge of the cliff'," *Federal Times*, March 21, 2013.

[8] "Uncle Sam Loses 4,900 Jobs in April," Government Executive, http://www.govexec.com/management/2013/05/uncle-sam-loses-4900-jobs-april/62969/.

[9] Joe Davidson, "Fallout from Recent Controversies Hurts Federal Workers," *Washington Post*, June 14, 2013.

[10] "Despite Freeze, Average Federal Salary Increases," *Washington Post,* April 10, 2013.

[11] U.S. Office of Personnel Management, 2012 Federal Employee Viewpoint Survey Results, November 2012.

[12] Tom Fox, "The Head Data Nerd," *Washington Post*, May 29, 2013.

[13] Davidson, June 14, 2013.

[14] Ibid.

[15] Ibid.

[16] Partnership for Public Service, "Federal Leaders Face Challenges Attracting Top College Graduates to Government Service, Partnership for Public Service," February 6, 2012.

Chapter 6

Strategies for Meeting Today's Challenges

Vision without execution is hallucination.

—Thomas A. Edison

Whether you be legislators, young people, or citizens in general, we are asking you to become aware of the need to *strengthen* the U.S. Civil Service for the good of our nation. We are asking you to realize that civil servants are our friends, not the enemy. They work for us, not against us. They provide services that we all need. As Americans, we are all on the same team, aren't we?

However, if we want to retain the services federal workers provide in the future, they need our support now—and we need to make our wishes known now, more than ever before. Toward the end of this chapter, we suggest some practical ways in which citizens can make their needs known.

Federal Work Is No Longer Honored—What Are Some Potential Remedies?

Federal Agencies Should Focus on Raising Awareness of— and Better Defending—the Value of What They Do and Why They Do It

Federal agencies have the responsibility to assertively describe why their work is valuable and why pursuing a career in federal service at their agencies is challenging and rewarding. They need to do a much better job of communicating the central importance of government service as the core of a more broadly defined understanding of public service. And if they are going to change public attitudes and begin to attract and retain the best and the brightest, they need to team up with the press to get agencies' *good* stories publicized—and they need to make this an urgent priority.

Agencies can fulfill these responsibilities more effectively than ever using new technologies that have become available over the last few years. Federal organizations, more than ever, have the ability to promote a better understanding of their programs, products, and services using web and social media, data visualization, and other types of IT innovation. They can get the word out about great job opportunities in their agencies and the increasingly valuable data dissemination and services available from the federal government today.

Best practices for government websites, covering web content, social media, and mobile apps, are provided by the website HowTo.gov, sponsored by the General Services Administration's Office of Citizen Services and Innovative Technologies and managed by the Federal Web Managers Council.

In addition, outreach opportunities for promoting their products and services in the press, on radio, and on television should be actively sought by the various communications offices of each respective agency. Instead of the national media outlets being used as a mallet for bashing feds, federal agencies need to make it a priority to take the initiative to create positive stories of what they do and why they do it and to get those stories out to the public across all media.

Prospective Hires and Those Involved in the Recruiting and Hiring Process Should Understand Not Just the Challenges but Also the Opportunities, Rewards, and Benefits of Federal Employment

Those considering federal employment should be aware of and support the attempts by federal agencies to attract, retain, and develop the strongest, most effective workforces possible. Following are a number of ways federal agencies are currently attempting to improve the recruitment, retention, and development of federal employees.

Increasing opportunities for internships are available nationwide. A critical and proven recruiting method is to improve student access to federal internships in all disciplines from high school to graduate school. Young people across this nation need encouragement in applying for federal jobs as a career choice. Their choice should be deliberate and not desperate. Many apply for federal jobs because of high unemployment rates. There are not many monetary rewards for federal service.

We do know that, to their great credit, Millennials (those born between 1980 and 2000) do value missions. Providing greater opportunity for young people to know and understand agency missions and potential careers will ultimately increase the pool of high-quality innovative and eager young people who choose federal jobs because they *want* a federal career. The federal government's internship program historically has lacked consistency across agencies and seemed to constantly change. Some agencies offer internship opportunities, whereas others do not.

There is a growing knowledge gap and declining expertise in many technical areas in the federal workforce because of retirements. Focused internship programs could alleviate this problem. There are still many careers that are highly technical that remain appropriate for the federal workforce rather than contractors. A recent example is the Gulf Coast oil spill and the need for technical expertise on how to stop it. Furthermore, many agencies may be overly relying on contractors for their IT knowledge. Many sensitive networks and databases are created and managed by private contractors.

Some systems are so crucial to U.S. national security that the hiring of federal employees for these sensitive positions might be more appropriate in terms of accountability, standardized system development, and maintenance. Federal internships could fill critical knowledge gaps and may also save federal spending over time by improving the long-term, consistent approach to IT system development and maintenance.

If you are a student in high school, college, or graduate school, you have a range of opportunities for government work. Agencies are using internships more and more as a gateway for new hires. The recently instituted Pathways program is intended to establish a standard, national way for students to enter federal careers from high school to after graduate school. According to the Pathways website,[1] as a student or recent graduate, an individual can begin his or her career in the federal government by choosing the path that best describes or fits personal academic pursuits:

- *Internship Program.* This program is for current students enrolled in a wide variety of educational institutions from high school to graduate level, with paid opportunities to work in agencies and explore federal careers while still in school.[2]
- *Recent Graduates Program.* This program is for individuals who have recently graduated from qualifying educational institutions or programs and are seeking a dynamic, career development program with training and mentorship. To be eligible, applicants must apply within two years of degree or certificate completion (except for veterans precluded from doing so due to their military service obligation, who will have up to six years to apply).[3]

Presidential Management Fellows Program. For more than three decades, the Presidential Management Fellows Program has been the federal government's premier leadership development program for advanced degree candidates. This program is now for individuals who have received a qualifying advanced degree within the preceding two years. For complete program information, visit http://www.pmf.gov/.

Current students also may want to explore virtual internships. These allow you to work for a government agency while still in school. Instead of leaving school, you take your assignments via e-mail or by webcam while working with a long-distance supervisor.

The opportunity to network and the overall experience gained from internships are valuable commodities that offer a competitive edge for hiring in agencies, with government contractors, and in the private and nonprofit sectors. Government service can make a difference.[4]

The Public Service Loan Forgiveness Program has been in place since 2007. The Federal Loan Repayment Program permits agencies to repay federally insured student loans as a recruitment or retention incentive for candidates or current employees of the agency.

http://www.opm.gov/policy-data-oversight/pay-leave/student-loan-repayment/.

This program may no longer be available as a recruitment tool for federal agencies. According to a *Washington Post* April 1, 2013 article, the House called for an end to this program in its budget plan.

http://www.washingtonpost.com/blogs/federal-eye/wp/2013/04/01/federal-employee-student-loan-repayment-program-targeted-for-repeal.

In 2007, Congress created the Public Service Loan Forgiveness Program to encourage individuals to enter into and/or to continue to work full time in public service jobs. Under this program, borrowers may qualify for forgiveness of the remaining balance due on their eligible federal student loans after they have made 120 payments on those loans under certain repayment plans while employed full time by certain public service employers.

http://www.studentaid.ed.gov/repay-loans/forgiveness-cancellation/charts/public-service#what-is-the-public.

Strong career enrichment and professional development and training programs exist in many federal agencies.

There are many ways in which agencies are enhancing employee development by helping staff to acquire specific competencies and obtain experience in a variety of agency areas. During these times of sequestration and cutbacks, training budgets are often the first to be reduced. However, agencies placing a high priority on the training of their federal employees are allocating protected training-specific funds in their annual budgets to protecting their commitment to their employees.

In addition, agencies' effective use of job rotations and stretch assignments within their respective organizations are helping employees to develop more well-rounded skill sets and is better preparing them for management and leadership positions in the future.

Teleworking opportunities abound in federal agencies. Young adults today have higher expectations for work–life balance. They value flexibility in their work arrangements—be it telecommuting, flexible hours, or part-time work. The signing of the Telework Enhancement Act in December 2010 served to provide a new and very important employee benefit as well as a way to improve agencies' organizational effectiveness.

Over the last two to three years, telework's improvement in work–life balance has been well documented. In addition, telework has improved the quality of life for the communities in which federal employees live and work, for example, by reducing traffic congestion and pollution. Certainly the advent of teleworking in federal agencies has become a powerful recruitment and retention tool with the capacity to improve the competitive position of the federal government for recruiting and retaining the best possible workforce.

If you are considering working for the federal government, we urge you to investigate telework and other opportunities for flexible work arrangements at the agencies in which you are interested. For starters, we suggest checking out the telework section on the OPM's website, http://www.opm.gov/, which includes information on how telework is enhancing the work–life balance and promoting management effectiveness in federal agencies.

Federal benefits are competitive for now—
Spread the word.

Congress created the Federal Employees Retirement System (FERS) in 1986, and it became effective on January 1, 1987. Since then, new federal civilian employees who have retirement coverage are covered by FERS.

To date, the FERS plan has provided a reliable way to ensure that federal workers will be able to retire with sufficient funds. Unlike the plans offered by many other organizations that provide only one source of benefit, such as a 401(k) plan or equivalent, FERS is a retirement plan that provides benefits to federal employees from three different sources: a Basic Benefit Plan, Social Security, and the Thrift Savings Plan (TSP).

The TSP part of FERS is an account that agencies automatically set up for eligible federal employees. Each pay period, the employee's agency deposits into her account an amount equal to 1 percent of the basic pay she earns for the pay period. Federal employees can also make their own contributions to their TSP accounts, and their agencies make matching contributions. The employee contributions are tax-deferred. The TSP is administered by the Federal Retirement Thrift Investment Board.

For more information about TSP, see their website at www.tsp.gov. See the Social Security Administration website www.ssa.gov for more information about the Social Security portion of federal employee retirement benefits. And more FERS information is available at www.opm.gov.

> The general public is responsible for guiding their congressional representatives to introduce legislation that holds federal agencies accountable and provides the necessary resources to carry out their missions.

The Public Should Become Better Informed about Services Provided by Federal Agencies and Urge Congress to Introduce Laws That Help Agencies to Do Their Jobs

We, as the taxpayers of this nation, have a duty to become an informed and engaged citizenry. Each of us should understand his important role and responsibility in the conduct of our own government provided to us by the federal government and why such services are important. Informed citizens would then appropriately support critical programs by contacting their congressional representatives to let them know which programs they support. The informed public would then voice support for the recruitment and training programs described in this chapter.

Change the conversation about federal employment and the federal workforce so that the young people will seek out career opportunities in federal service. The general public can and should encourage Congress and the White House to introduce legislation that supports federal agencies that provide needed services. There should also be informed debate about programs that have outlived their useful lives. After an honest debate, an informed citizenry would then be able vote their voice.

Of course, Congress can be difficult to follow. If you want to voice your concerns to Congress, what are some practical ways that you can do this? We suggest, for starters, that you go to a website called OpenCongress (www.opencongress.com). On this site, you can track issues you care about, among them issues affecting federal workers.

You can subscribe to RSS feeds or e-mail updates on bills, votes, issues, and so forth. Via the tools provided on this site, you can make your voice heard. OpenCongress gives you tools to contact Congress and open a dialogue with your elected officials. On this site you can vote "aye" or "nay" on bills, give personal approval ratings to members of Congress, post comments in discussion forums, and write your members of Congress directly.

So what else can you do? There are, indeed, other ways that you can lend your support to initiatives for restoring honor to the U.S. Civil

Service. For example, former Federal Reserve chairman Paul Volcker, a veteran of several government reform commissions, recently launched a group to restore trust in government.

The Volcker Alliance "seeks to rekindle intellectual, practical, and academic interest in the implementation of policy—the 'nuts and bolts' of government—and serve as a catalyst for sustained government improvement," he said in the organization's mission statement. "There is an urgent need to restore trust and pride in the way our public institutions implement policies—from the White House and Congress to statehouses, cities, and towns across our country and in democracies around the world," as well as how "private initiatives and incentives can be allied with public purpose."[5]

> As civil service departments and agencies achieve successes in their respective missions, they should publicize these good stories, and do so on a frequent basis.

Shelley Metzenbaum, a former Office of Management and Budget leader and founding president of the Volcker Alliance, stated the top goals for the Volcker Alliance in a *Washington Post* interview for the Federal Coach published on August 7, 2013. According to Metzenbaum, "we're focusing on effective execution of public policy and rebuilding public trust in government. We plan to work as a catalyst for change in alliance with educational institutions, government, business and nonprofit groups. . . . Debate about smarter policies gets attention from the best minds, and government problems get everyone's attention. We want the best minds also giving serious attention to the challenge of implementing policies and to enabling people to be great government implementors."[6]

Another example of a group that seeks to improve the workings of the federal government is the Government Transformation Initiative (GTI). Headed by David Walker, the former head of the Government Accountability Office (GAO), the GTI is a coalition of corporations and nonprofit organizations with the stated mission of improving the economy, efficiency, effectiveness, and credibility of federal operations and programs. According to Walker, the commission is needed because there currently is no entity dedicated entirely to improving government operations and management. While GAO issues reports on government operations issues, including its annual list of high risk government programs in need of improvement, it does not provide specific recommendations to Congress on how to fix the problems it identifies.

Walker also noted that the Government Transformation Commission would supplement the work of Congress, which he said does not spend as much time as it should on issues involving government operations. He said, "Establishing such a commission would improve Congress and the president an entity dedicated entirely towards improving government operations and management, resulting in significant federal savings and improved performance."[7] Walker noted that the commission would supplement the work of Congress, which he said does not spend as much time as it should on issues involving government operations.

This bipartisan commission is now in the form of legislation in both the House and the Senate. On

July 11, 2013, Representative Cheri Bustos (D-IL) and eleven cosponsors of both parties introduced the Government Transformation Act (H.R. 2675) to empanel a commission of seven nonfederal employees to hold hearings, coordinate with agencies, issue regular reports to Congress, and propose management reforms that would be translated into legislative language and given up-or-down votes in Congress.

On July 1, 2013, Senator Mark Kirk (R-IL) introduced a similar bill (S. 1297). Walker also noted that by implementing cost-savings measures, the federal government would have more fiscal flexibility for needed investments while, at the same time, helping to restore fiscal sanity. Establishing a Government Transformation Commission would also send a signal to the public that action is being taken, in a bipartisan manner, to help restore confidence in the Federal government.[8]

And yet another effort to define and articulate a set of reforms for the federal government is a report titled "Building the Enterprise: Nine Strategies for a More Integrated, Effective Government," authored by the Partnership for Public Service and Booz, Allen, Hamilton.[9] The recommendations in this report "focus on a central premise: Our government must take a more coordinated, multi-agency, whole-of-government approach—in other words, an enterprise approach—to the nation's most difficult and enduring challenges." The goal is "leading and managing the entire civil service system as an integrated enterprise—with a cross-cutting strategy, management infrastructure, and leadership."

As civil service departments and agencies achieve successes in their respective missions, and make progress in cooperation with such improvement efforts as the Volcker Alliance, the Government Transformation Initiative, and the Building the Enterprise recommendations, they should publicize these good stories, and do so on a frequent basis.

To be sure, in 2013, sequestration and the nation's financial troubles are currently taking a toll on federal government employees. Although the conventional wisdom now seems to be that sequestration isn't as bad as expected, defense and nondefense agencies alike are truly feeling the effects of the sequester furloughs and trimmed contracts, and travel and training budgets are slowly but surely deteriorating the federal government's ability to perform its mission. The budget uncertainties make work very hard to manage for America.

Remember that these sequestration cuts are being imposed in part so that Congress can avoid making decisions about *real* fiscal reforms that add revenues and reduce the costs of big programs like Medicare and Social Security. Now is the time for we the people to let our concerns known.

Let your members of Congress know that they must provide a realistic budget for the nation. If you would like to make your views on sequestration and other critical issues of the federal government known to those who can change the status quo, you can contact your representative in the U.S. House of Representatives and/or contact one or both of your state's senators in the U.S. Senate.

To find and contact your congressional district's representatives, go to
http://www.house.gov/representatives/find.

To find your state's senators, go to

http://www.senate.gov/general/contact_individual_senators_cfm.cfm.

To contact your senators, go to http://www.senators/reference/common/faq/How_to_contact_senators.htm.

It is also possible to make your views on sequestration known to the White House via http://www.whitehouse.gov/contact. Please make sure that you mention that you do not agree with people who make federal employees the scapegoat for everything—that you believe that is wrong. Please ask Congress to do their job and reach a fair and honest compromise, and to get it done in a way that protects the federal workforce that serves our nation.

Notes to Chapter 6

[1] https://www.usajobs.gov/StudentsAndGrads.

[2] Additional information about the internship program can be found at http://www.opm.gov/policy-data-oversight/hiring-authorities/students-recent-graduates/#url=Program-Fact-Sheets.

[3] See tp://www.opm.gov/policy-data-oversight/hiring-authorities/students-recent-graduates/#url=Program-Fact-Sheets.

[4] To find internship opportunities, go to http://www.usa.gov/ and http://www.usajobs.gov/ and do separate keyword searches on these words: *intern, internships, student, student employment, volunteer, fellowship, pathways,* and *virtual internship.*

[5] http://volckeralliance.com/.

[6] Tom Fox, "Rebuilding Trust," Washington Post, August 7, 2013.

[7] David M. Walker, Testimony before U.S. House of Representatives Committee on Oversight and Government Reform Hearing: Reinventing Government, June 18, 2013.

[8] Ibid.

[9] Partnership for Public Service and Booz, Allen, Hamilton, *Building the Enterprise: Nine Strategies for a More Integrated, Effective Government,*

August 2013, http://ourpublicservice.org/OPS/publications/viewcontentdetails.php?id=228.

Chapter 7

Develop and Attract the Next Generation of Civil Service Leaders

> Focusing your life solely on making a buck shows a certain poverty of ambition. It asks too little of yourself. Because it's only when you hitch your wagon to something larger than yourself that you realize your true potential.
> —Barack Obama

We might ask ourselves, what will become of the U.S. Civil Service if our country can't attract and retain the best leaders to guide us to our future?

Today, the United States is facing daunting challenges in all aspects of the federal government, and a highly capable group of senior civil servant leaders is needed to implement critical initiatives. That's where the Senior Executive Service (SES) comes in. So why is the SES important? And what does the SES do?

Comprising primarily career positions, the SES was designed to be largely insulated from political influence but was intended to provide a consistent source of leadership across administrations. Leaders in the SES are invaluable because they provide the mission critical continuity that transcends the tenure of political appointees. The SES corps, operating and overseeing nearly every government activity across almost seventy-five agencies, serves as the link between these political appointees and the rest of the federal workforce—in effect, it is the glue that holds the government together.

A big problem is emerging, though. Today, more and more mid-level managers are questioning whether getting into the SES is worth the potentially negative effects on their work–life balance or lack of control over where they might be assigned to work.[1] And among SES members, there is a marked decline in those who would agree that SES pay and benefits are helpful in attracting high-level senior executives.[2]

> Today, more and more mid-level managers are questioning whether getting into the SES is worth the potentially negative effects on their work–life balance or lack of control over where they might be assigned to work.

To be sure, with the serious SES pay compression that exists today, a GS-15 step 10 can be making more money than his SES boss. Even for those highly motivated to better serve the American people, it gives many GS-14 or GS-15 federal employees pause before they apply to the SES ranks.

The risk–reward ratio is skewed, leading many to determine that they would rather remain in the GS than take on an SES job. I (Mark) can tell you that over the last few years, as I met with GS-15s reporting to me for performance evaluations and to discuss their future plans, more than one of them told me, more than once, that they did not want to apply for an SES position. They asked why should they, when at best, the pay difference they would receive is not nearly proportionate to the increase in the workload, responsibility, and risk associated with an SES position. It is a good question.

Indeed, data drawn from the Partnership for

Public Service Study Best Places to Work rankings, based on the Office of Personnel Management's (OPM's) 2012 Federal Employee Viewpoint Survey, show that federal leadership is on the decline. The report states that "while federal employees have not given high marks to their leaders for years, satisfaction with leadership dropped in 2012 for the first time since the Best Places to Work rankings were published in 2003."

Overall, the leadership score was 52.8 on a 100-point scale, a drop of 2.1 points from 2011. That doesn't sound like much, but "it is definitely significant and consequential," said Max Stier, the Partnership's president and chief executive officer. "The decrease in satisfaction with senior leaders is especially worrisome," the report said. The effective leadership of senior managers is "the largest driver of employee satisfaction and commitment."[3]

During times like these, when the overarching issue in Congress is the pressing need to pass a budget (or else sequestration will remain in place absent public outcry), we believe that federal agencies, more than ever, need strong leaders who can communicate the value of what they do and why they do it. They need to communicate this to their own employees as well as to the tax-paying public. Yet, today, it is disturbing that signs point to a senior leadership in decline.

It's Hard for Federal Agencies to Attract and Retain Quality Employees at the Senior Executive Service Level

At the end of 2012, approximately 64 percent of the nearly seventy-one hundred senior executives were eligible to retire by 2016.[4] And more and more, they are beginning to seriously consider retiring. According to the OPM, the percentage of SES members who retired by the end of 2009 was 5.8 percent. This was up to 8.3 percent by the end of 2012, and the flow of candidates to fill up the pipeline to replace retiring senior executives is not keeping up with agencies' needs.

It takes special talent to become a member of the SES. Not only must an aspiring executive have exceptional technical skills in the chosen field, but the individual must also know how to lead others, manage complicated programs, and in some cases oversee massive budgets. But many senior agency officials are complaining that the candidates they now receive don't have what it takes. And rather than accept a substandard executive, agencies are forced to look all over again before finding the right person for the job, wasting valuable time and limited resources.

It is not unusual to post position announcements twice, maybe even more often than that. Agency officials cite a wide range of problems, including shortsighted training and succession planning that must be corrected to overcome the lack of qualified candidates. And while agencies keep looking for someone to fill a position, they have to rely on acting officials, who often don't have the power to make budgetary or strategic decisions, to keep operations in a holding pattern.[5]

Taking the Helm?

Sensing this problem early on, in July 2009, the Senior Executives Association issued an open call for GS-14/15 employees to respond to an online survey. Survey questions solicited information on respondents' views and interests concerning career SES positions. The survey results revealed that the SES has become less attractive to senior GS-14 and GS-15 employees than it was in the past.[6] According to the survey, the most significant detractors for considering an SES position were the following:

1. *Work–life balance.* Senior executives take on more duties and work longer hours, yet receive no compensatory time, no locality pay, and no guaranteed annual cost-of-living pay raise, all of which GS employees receive.

2. *Pay compression.* All pay raises for senior executives are based on performance. In addition, senior executives are not eligible for overtime or locality pay. The resulting pay overlap between SES and upper-level GS-14 and -15 employees reduces the financial incentive for GS employees to apply for the SES.

3. *Change of geographic relocation.* The SES was meant to be a corps of leaders who would periodically move within and across agencies and sectors to gain an enterprise-wide perspective. Today, however, the risk of geographic reassignment is seen as a deterrent to joining the SES.

Congress Should Strengthen, Not Weaken, the Ability of Federal Agencies to Perform Their Missions

Another detractor to those qualified individuals

aspiring to SES positions has emerged in the form of a recent spate of congressional bills that have attacked SES performance awards.[7] A recent column in the Senior Executives Association newsletter, *ACTION*, states,

> "The attacks on SES awards have been insidious, wide-spread and ongoing for the past several years. These attacks have now reached the point where, especially in the context of a sequestration environment, SES awards are becoming increasingly at risk. . . . Considering that we are now in the third year of a pay freeze and the fact that the SES is not eligible for within-grade increases, overtime pay, compensatory time or locality pay, performance awards are the only current means an agency has to make meaningful distinctions based on relative performance. . . . Also an agency should be able to recognize the exceptional performance of many Senior Executives and any federal employee for that matter who, under difficult conditions, accomplishes truly amazing results in very challenging times. The annual performance award was one means of doing this."[8]

Legislation has recently been introduced (S. 986) that would prohibit all SES performance awards as long as the sequestration continues. However, eroding the pay- for- performance system is not the kind of serious reform that will improve the SES system. It will certainly leave the SES increasingly undesirable for both current and aspiring senior executives.

Certainly, it is understood that many such bills were introduced in the wake of the General Services Administration's scandal of 2012. But that scandal, as heinous as it was, was limited to just a few poorly behaving individuals, and we believe it shouldn't be used by Congress to make an example of people who have not engaged in wrongdoing. This treatment of senior executives by our national leaders focuses on the negative, on distrust, is just unfair, and mistreats the overwhelming majority of SESers who are conscientious and doing a great job.

As they did in the past, performance awards should be used to recognize accomplishments and results, for coaching to encourage responsible risk taking, and for building trust leading to improved performance. However, today, all too often, the SES performance system focuses on negative incentives such as withholding bonuses or reducing pay to dispense discipline after something goes wrong. In any event, prohibiting or diminishing SES awards lessens the ability to promote the SES as an elite corps dedicated to excellence. We urge you to contact members of Congress about the positive effects of performance awards and why legislation prohibiting or limiting these awards is counterproductive to good government.

Another piece of legislation negatively affecting the SES ranks, the Government Employee Accountability Act, introduced by Representative Mike Kelly (R-PA) and which passed the House last year, would allow agencies to place SES members on "investigative leave without pay" before being found guilty of misconduct. Remarking on this bill in the *Washington Post*, Federal Diary, on July 23, 2013, Carol A. Bonosaro, president of the Senior

Executives Association, said, "To the uninformed, Rep. Kelly's bill sounds sensible, however, Senior Executives already serve at considerable risk since they have virtually no effective appeal rights. The bill would create a 'guilty until proven innocent' standard."[9]

Repealing a Provision of the STOCK Act: A Good Thing

We do commend Congress and the president for recently passing a bill to prevent financial disclosure forms filed by many senior career federal employees from being posted online in a searchable, sortable database. In April 2013, Congress passed a bill that indefinitely delayed and effectively repealed a controversial provision of the STOCK Act which had been enacted in April 2012.[10]

> The Senior Executive Service Reform Act of 2012 was intended to improve the SES by helping to attract, retain, develop and reward our nation's most talented civil servants . . . It is expected that this bill will be re-introduced as part of the 113th Congress.

The provision in question would have required that federal agencies post online the financial disclosure forms of about twenty-eight thousand of their employees—including all employees in the SES. This would have put select federal employees at higher potential risk for identity theft and other crimes and would have resulted in having to accept higher security risks for the government. Obviously, if this provision had prevailed, it certainly would have discouraged prospective candidates from aspiring to the SES ranks. "It [the 2013 bill] doesn't use the word 'repeal,' but in our eyes it's basically the same thing," said Jenny Mattingley, director of government affairs for the Senior Executives Association. "It's not going into effect. For us, it's encouraging."[11]

Reintroduce the Senior Executive Service Reform Act of 2012

We also urge Congress and the administration, and those in the voting general public who elect these leaders, to support *positive* bills that promote the strengthening of the SES corps. One example of such a bill is the Senior Executive Service Reform Act of 2012, introduced during the course of the 112th Congress.[12] This bill was about much more than SES compensation. It included a call for a number of reforms to: career management, the SES hiring process, and increasing diversity within the SES, as well as to improving SES compensation.

It is expected that this bill will be re-introduced as part of the 113th Congress, and we need you to contact Congress and voice your support for it. Following is a summary of reforms called for by the bill:

Improve SES Career Management

Codify an SES Resource Office within OPM to improve the efficiency, effectiveness, productivity, and professionalism of the SES, preventing a future administration from eliminating it.
Increase the transparency of SES rating

systems by requiring agencies to provide senior executives with their rating level and an explanation for the rating level within thirty days of giving the rating.

Strengthen agencies' Candidate Development Programs (CDPs). Only 11 percent of career SES members, as of March 2011, graduated from a CDP. The bill requires agencies to align CDPs to succession planning, improving the rotational experience and assigning mentors to CDP participants.

Improve agency onboarding programs by requiring each agency, in consultation with OPM, to establish an onboarding program for newly appointed career and non-career senior executives.

Reform the SES Hiring Process

Ensure applicants have sufficient time to apply for vacancies by specifying a time period for job listings. The bill also eliminates the Executive Core Qualification narratives for the initial stage of the application and instead allows applicants to submit a cover letter and, résumé, and to answer brief questions.

> Interestingly, almost every Fortune 500 company teaches emotional intelligence. It is the only thing you can affect as a leader and should be the foundation for all federal employees and leaders.

Increase Diversity within the SES
Promote diversity within the SES by requiring each agency to submit to OPM a plan, updated every two years, to maximize opportunities for the appointment of minorities, women, and individuals with disabilities to the SES.

This bill was sponsored by Senator Akaka (D-HI) in the Senate and Congressman Jim Moran (D-VA) in the House. Cosponsors of the bill were: Representative. Gerry Connolly (D-VA), Representative, Chris Van Hollen (D-MD), and Delegate Eleanor Holmes Norton. The bill is supported by the Senior Executives Association and the Partnership for Public Service. New Senate sponsors need to be identified as Senator Akaka retired at the end of 2012.

> We tend to bring in outside consultants to drive and disperse innovation. They can help guide a conversation, but change that sticks has to be an inside job.

Other Ways to Improve Federal Leadership in General

In addition to supporting the many important measures of the Senior Executive Service Reform Act of 2012, there are other ways to support and improve the leadership of federal employees. Various such strategies were discussed by Tom Fox, author of the "Federal Coach" column for the *Washington Post,* in an April 2013 interview of Brigadier General John Michel, an organizational change expert. Agencies can help their employees increase performance by taking steps to increase the development of the emotional intelligence of their leaders.

Brigadier General Michel states that

> emotional intelligence (EQ) is the other kind of smart. It refers to the ability to perceive, control and evaluate emotions so we can maximize our positive interactions with others. Leaders with high EQ are true treasures in the workplace, because they have strong interpersonal skills. They offer and ask helpful questions and mitigate conflict productively. When it comes to job performance, EQ counts for up to 60 percent of an individual's performance compared with IQ, which is fixed when we are very young, and personality, which is fixed by the time we're 20. Interestingly, almost every Fortune 500 company teaches emotional intelligence. It is the only thing you can affect as a leader and should be a foundation for all Federal employees and leaders.[13]

In response to a question on how federal leaders can energize the employees they lead, Michel further stated,

> *Leaders must be cognizant about how they show up to the workplace every day.* They need to ask, "'How can I be a role model that's going to live the message that we are trying to send?"' Bringing that positive sense of self to work and doing intentional little things to communicate you want to help bring out the best in your people is powerful. To

put a spin on Gandhi's phrase, lead the change you want to see by setting an example worth emulating.[14]

Michel also spoke about how federal agencies can help their employees to be innovative and creative:

> *We need to liberate employees to solve problems in compelling and creative ways.* When we equip, encourage, and empower people to believe they can do something significant, they will rise to the occasion. Finally, we must stop relying on easy "'one-size-fits-all'" solutions. We tend to bring in outside consultants to drive and disperse innovation. They can help guide a conversation, but change that sticks has to be an inside job.[15]

An Organization Is Only as Good as Its People

Speaking of consultants and outside contractors, we'd like to conclude with a plea to the government to stop outsourcing its work. We say this because we see a troublesome pattern emerging. Over the past ten to fifteen years, there has been an increased reliance on government contractors. As agencies increasingly looked to outside sources of expertise instead of developing talent from within the civil service ranks, we have seen a decaying in the quality of executive and technical talent and widespread morale problems within government.

As a first step in countering this disturbing trend, we urge each agency to redouble their efforts to identify what they should never outsource; to ensure that the agencies are not contracting out their core mission nor detrimentally impacting the safety and security of the people of this great nation. Agencies should more carefully identify criteria for determining what operations make sense to outsource and when it makes sense to remain in-house. It is much more cost effective, in terms of continuity of resources and key operations, for federal agencies to nurture their inside talent, not drive it away.

Notes for Chapter 7

[1] Senior Executives Association and Avue Technologies Corporation, *Taking the Helm: Attracting the Next Generation of Federal Leaders,* October 2010; used with written consent.

[2] U.S. Office of Personnel Management, "Senior Executive Service Survey Results for Fiscal Year 2011," U.S. Office of Personnel Management, May 2012.

[3] Partnership for Public Service, "The Best Places to Work in the Federal Government: 2012 Rankings," December 2012.

[4] Senator Daniel K. Akaka (D-HI) and Rep. James M. Moran (D-VA), Senior Executive Service Reform Act of 2012, June 2012.

[5] "Why So Many SES Jobs Go Unfilled," *Federal Times*, September 13, 2010.

[6] Senior Executives Association and Avue Technologies Corporation, October 2010.

[7] Senior Executives Association, ACTION, Washington, DC, Volume 33, No. 3, (March 2013) (used with written permission).

[8] Senior Executives Association, ACTION, Washington, DC, Volume 33, No. 6, (June 2013) (used with written permission).

[9] Joe Davidson, "Panel to Vote on Bills that Target Federal Workers," *Washington Post*, July 23, 2013.

[10] Stop Trading on Congressional Knowledge Act ("STOCK" Act), Pub. L. 112-105, S. 2038, 126 Stat. 291, enacted April 4, 2012).

[11] Eric Yoder, "Congress Blocks Online Postings of Financial Disclosure," *Washington Post*, April 15, 2013.

[12] Akaka and Moran, Senior Executive Service Reform Act of 2012, June 2012.

[13] Tom Fox, "Pushing Past Mediocrity in the Federal Workplace," *Washington Post*, April 16, 2013.

[14] Ibid.

[15] Ibid.

Epilogue

Without question, 2013 was a challenging year for civil servants. There was sequestration, plus ongoing budget cuts and pay freezes. Then, Congress shut down a large portion of the federal government for three weeks in October, furloughing hundreds of thousands of employees. They did this because they were not able to pass a bill, in a timely manner, to fund the federal government due to political infighting.

Congress' political failures were damaging to the federal workforce. Those elected to serve us failed to do their jobs. And federal workers were found guilty by association with the federal bureaucracy as a whole, being blamed for the failures of our political leaders.

Civil servants have chosen to work for the federal government because they want to make a difference. We fear, given recent events, that federal jobs might not look very attractive to prospective new employees. However, there might be a ray of hope on the horizon for the up-and-coming generation that might be considering federal employment. For example, we saw, as the partial government shutdown continued through the first weeks of October, that the public's perception of federal employees actually improved. The longer the shutdown lasted, the more the public began to miss the services civil servants provide and the less they approved the performance of Congress.

Representative Jason Chaffetz (R-Utah) said, "there's wide recognition that it's not the federal employee's fault. For your rank-and-file federal worker, there is a lot of sympathy for them getting caught up in the pig sty that is Washington, D.C. Everybody is sympathetic to that."

Well we're not sure that everybody is sympathetic to the plight of the federal worker, but perhaps this is at least a step or two in the right direction. We hope that our writing (and your reading) of this book also will help to advance the cause of the civil servant. We hope that the up-and-coming generation will be increasingly encouraged to pursue federal service as a career and that those aspiring to leadership positions in the SES will see, with new legislation in the offing, that help is on the way.

It is time, today, to again put forward federal government service as a worthy calling for U.S. citizens. In doing so, there are important roles to be played and responsibilities to be undertaken by an informed public, federal agencies, and our political leaders.

To effectively do our part in a democracy, we must become an informed citizenry. An informed citizenry holds its elected officials accountable. A truly informed citizenry has a working knowledge of, and, it is hoped, an appreciation for, the federal services they receive and for the federal employees who provide those services.

Federal agencies certainly have important roles and responsibilities of their own to raise awareness of the value of what they do and why they do it. Today, more than ever, each agency should persuasively state why its mission and initiatives are valuable to the nation, why pursuing a civil service career with the agency is a worthy calling, and the benefits of working for the agency. Each agency should also more aggressively defend its employees against unfair attacks from politicians and the press.

Max Stier, president and CEO of the Partnership for Public Service, in a *Washington Post* op-ed titled "Give Public Servants the Recognition—and Pay—They Deserve," stated, "While our government must deal forthrightly with its problems, we will never get the government we want and need if we continually demonize it or fail to value those who dedicate themselves to public service."[1]

We believe that, unfortunately, federal employees will continue to be unfairly vilified by some in the media and Congress. For this reason, federal agencies and their employees must be defended against these unfair attacks.

You can help. Don't pile on with those who disparage federal employees out of ignorance. Don't blame federal employees for budget problems they did not create. Instead, be aware of the valuable civil services you receive each day and speak well of the civil servants who provide them. Communicate with your representatives and let them know your concerns and compliment the work of the civil servants who provide good public services to you. As a responsible citizen of our great democracy, begin holding elected officials accountable to do the jobs you elected them to do.

When did "we the people" give up our power? Remember, we are regular citizens, too, and we were civil servants. It is worth repeating—all of us must become aware of what the U.S. Civil Servant does for us and for our fellow citizens every day. Tell your congressional representatives that you support government-wide and agency-led improvements for providing even better civil services—for improving *your* civil services of today and tomorrow, for the good of the United States of America.

Learn and speak the facts about federal employment and the federal workforce so that the young people around you will be encouraged to seek out career opportunities in federal service. In fostering success in civil service careers, be assured that you will be doing much to promote the success of our nation, today and tomorrow.

So, where does all this leave us? The sequestration, which began to take place in March 2013, cut $85 billion from the federal budget for fiscal year 2013. Had these government-wide spending reductions continued there would have been successively deeper cuts of about $109 billion a year, amounting to $1 trillion in agency budget cuts through 2021.

Congress and the White House ultimately agreed to a budget deal which maintained some of the planned cuts and increased the cost of retirement benefits for new federal employees. As the shutdown came to a close in mid-October 2013, the president and some in Congress said that the government would not be shut down again. That is true for now.

As this book goes to print, government funding will not expire on January 15, 2014. We hope this means there is a change to our leadership's perspective of its federal employees. Maybe now civil service will return to be considered an honorable profession as it should have been all along.

We will see. Stay tuned. And get involved.

Note to Epilogue

Max Stier, "Give Public Servants the Recognition—and Pay—They Deserve," *Washington Post,* May 16, 2013.

Appendix: Informative Websites

This appendix contains a list of websites providing information about U.S. government departments and agencies.

http://www.usa.gov/, *The U.S. Government's Official Web Portal*
Find information by topic for citizen, business, and nonprofit concerns; government employees; and visitors to the United States

http://www.usa.gov/directory/federal, *A–Z Index of U.S. Government Departments and Agencies*
This site lists all the departments and agencies of the U.S. government in one place, alphabetically.

Fedstats.gov
FedStats provides easy access to statistics and information produced by more than one hundred U.S. federal government agencies available to citizens everywhere.

http://www.gsa.gov/, *Federal Citizen Information Center—GSA*

The Office of the Federal Citizen Information Center (FCIC) provides U.S. government information and services directly to the public. It currently offers a variety of information channels, websites, web chat, telephone, print, social media, and e-mail. FCIC programs include GobiernoUSA.gov—its mobile site and apps gallery are Spanish-language counterparts to USA.gov.

Blog.USA.gov
This site showcases the helpfulness and practicality of federal, state, and local government information.

Kids.gov
This is a portal to government websites designed especially for kids and educators.

BusinessUSA.gov
This is the U.S. government's official web portal to support business start-ups, growth, financing, and exporting.

Data.gov
This site increases public access to high value, machine-readable data sets generated by the executive branch of the federal government.

DisasterAssistance.gov
A place where citizens, emergency responders, and government officials can find the latest domestic disaster-related news, information, and resources.

E-Gov.com
Find out how federal employees are serving citizens, businesses, and local communities via e-government.

GOVLoans.gov
Your gateway to government loan information. It directs you to the loan information that best meets your needs.

Grants.gov
Your source to find information on more than one

thousand grant programs. By registering once on Grants.gov, your organization can apply for grants from the twenty-six federal agencies that annually award more than $400 billion.

USASpending.gov
A website providing the public with information about how their tax dollars are spent.

Bibliography

Bilmes, Linda J., and W. Scott Gould, *The People Factor: Strengthening America by Investing in Public Service.* Washington, D.C.: Brookings Institution Press, 2009.

Deming, W. Edwards. *Out of the Crisis.* Cambridge, Mass.: MIT Press, 1986.

Donahue, John D. *The Warping of Government Work.* Cambridge, Mass.: Harvard University Press, 2008.

Holzer, Mark, ed. *Public Service: Callings, Commitments, and Contributions.* Oxford: Westview Press, 2000.

Martínez -Lorente, Angel R., et.al, Total Quality Management: Origins and Evolution of the Term, 1998.

About the Authors

Deborah Johnson had more than twenty years of experience with freight, international, and maritime-related data and analysis. She served as acting deputy director, assistant director for transportation analysis, and senior transportation specialist of the Bureau of Transportation Statistics of the Research and Innovative Technology Administration, U.S. Department of Transportation. In this capacity, she managed day-to-day operations and led a team of professionals who performed research and provided technical support in a variety of areas, including transportation system performance, passenger travel, freight transportation, transportation safety and environmental impacts, and other domestic and international transportation trends, issues, and data.

**Mark Wallace** began his federal career at the U.S. Census Bureau in 1976 and worked on economic censuses and current surveys until he retired in 2012. As a member of the Senior Executive Service for more than a decade, he was a well-known and respected international expert in the collection and dissemination of service sector statistics. He led the introduction and expansion of annual and quarterly surveys of service industries, measuring service sectors covered previously only every five years in the Economic Census, greatly improving estimates of U.S. economic growth. Mark received the Department of Commerce's bronze medal in 1985, the silver medal in 1997, and the gold medal in 2011.

Deborah and Mark first met in 2006. They were co-project leaders of a major report on U.S. transportation activity, the Commodity Flow Survey, undertaken through a partnership between the Census Bureau and the Bureau of Transportation Statistics. They also served together as leaders of the North American Transportation Statistics Interchange, a trilateral forum of government officials from transportation and statistical agencies of the United States, Canada, and Mexico. They both retired in 2012.

www.ingramcontent.com/pod-product-compliance
Lightning Source LLC
Chambersburg PA
CBHW051809170526
45167CB00005B/1940